Gemini

Gemini

MAY 22–JUNE 21

*Your Sun-and-Moon Guide
to Love and Life*

Ronnie Dreyer

Ariel Books

**Andrews McMeel
Publishing**

Kansas City

Gemini: Your Sun-and-Moon Guide to Love and Life copyright © 1997 by Armand

Eisen. All rights reserved. Printed in the United States of America. No part

of this book may be used or reproduced in any manner whatsoever without

written permission except in the case of reprints in the context of reviews.

For information write Andrews McMeel Publishing, an Andrews McMeel

Universal company, 4520 Main Street, Kansas City, Missouri 64111.

www.andrewsmcmeel.com

Interior artwork by Robyn Officer

ISBN: 0-8362-3560-6

Library of Congress Catalog Card Number: 97-71542

Contents

Contents

Contents

Contents

Gemini

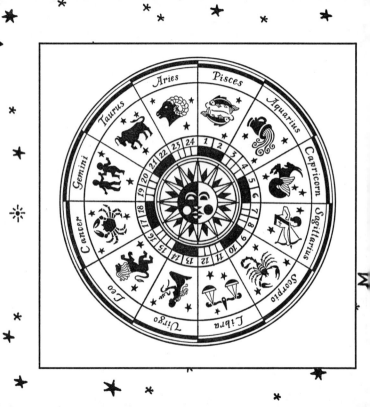

Introduction

How, *you ask, might*
astrology make a difference in your life,
in your mental, emotional, and spiritual

growth? Of course, there is no single answer to this question, for the responses are as diverse as humanity itself. Some of us may wish to dabble, enjoying astrology as we would a new hobby; have some fun; check out our sign and the signs of our friends, lovers, and children; and muse over the romantic possibilities of various combinations. What, for example, are the chances that a Libra man and a Pisces woman would hit it off? Others of us might wish to embark on a lifelong adventure, plumbing the depths of esoteric wisdom and emerging with startling new revelations about ourselves and our lives. Whatever your interest, you will find that astrology has something for everyone.

Astrology, which began as a search for a pattern in the cosmos, is based on the relationship between the infinitely large and the infinitely small, between the macrocosm—primarily our solar system, with its Sun, Moon, and planets, but also the fixed stars beyond—and the microcosm, the mysterious individual personality. In other words, astrology is the study of how celestial bodies influence the Earth and affect the human beings who dwell here.

In this regard, it's important to understand that astrology deals with symbols. The signs of the zodiac represent powerful forces, profound energies of the mind, heart, and soul. These energies are expressed in our personal horoscope, or birth chart, which describes the position of the heavens at our moment of birth and therefore portrays our unique personalities, our likes and dislikes, our strengths and weaknesses, our hopes and fears.

A horoscope is not, however, a simple reading of the future, a trip to the fortune-teller. You might want to consider your horoscope as a kind of map, indicating, say, the model of car you are driving, the condition of its motor, the state of the road (which may be bumpy in some places and smooth in others), and the variety of spiritual and emotional terrain you are likely to encounter during your life's journey. Perhaps the motor needs a tune-up; perhaps two roads pass through a particular stretch of wilderness, one road potholed and poor, the other sure and clear; perhaps just off the beaten path lies a great marvel you would miss if you didn't know it was there. What you do with the map astrology provides is up to you: You are free to choose, free to act as you will, free to make the most of your life—and, too, free to have plenty of fun along the way.

A Brief
History

*L*ong *ago, men and* women looked up into the starry night sky and wondered what it was and what effect it had on their lives. From that first primordial inquiry, astrology was born. No one quite knows how far back astrology's oral tradition extends; its first appearance in recorded history dates to 2500 B.C. in ancient Mesopotamia, where it was believed that the heavenly bodies were great gods with powers to influence the course of human affairs. Those early astrologers began to observe the heavens carefully and keep systematic records of what they saw in the great glittering silence of the night sky. The royal family's astrological counselors advised them on how to rule; early in its history, astrology was considered the "royal art."

The ancient Greeks already boasted

an ample pantheon of gods by the time their astronomers began to use the new science of geometry to explain the workings of the heavens. The Greeks combined Mesopotamia's form of astrological divination with their own mythology and the new science of geometry, developing a personal astrology based on the zodiac—from the Greek *zodiakos kyklos*, or "circle of animals"—a belt extending nine degrees on either side of the ecliptic, the Sun's apparent annual path across the sky. The belt was divided into segments named after animals—the Ram, the Bull, the Crab—and set to correspond to certain dates of the year. The Greeks were thus able to use astrology to counsel individuals who were curious about the effect of the heavens on their lives; the art of reading personal horoscopes was born.

As one seer of the times said, speaking of the heavens, "There is no speech nor language where their voice is not heard." Astrology was incorporated into Roman culture and spread with the extension of the Roman Empire throughout Europe. With the rise of Christianity, astrology faced a challenge: After all, it seemed to suggest that humans were determined by the stars, rather than by the stars' creator, who also, according to emerging Christian theology, had granted humans free will. Generally, however, astrology was absorbed into Christian teachings and continued to flourish; witness the selection of an astrological date for Christmas. Like much of classical culture, astrology went into decline during the Middle Ages, emerging in the early Renaissance to occupy a privileged place in the world of learning; in the sixteenth and seventeenth centuries, it was embraced by the prominent astronomers

Tycho Brahe and Johannes Kepler and was taught as a science in Europe's great universities.

Eventually, the discoveries of modern science began to erode the widely held belief in astrology's absolute scientific veracity. In our times, though, astrology remains as popular as ever, as an alternative to scientific theory, and as a way for people to articulate the manifold richness of the self. Psychologist Carl

Jung noted that astrology "contains all the wisdom of antiquity"; for modern men and women in search of the soul, it holds perennial interest as an expression of the psyche's mysterious relationship to the myriad wonders of the universe.

The Heavens

An Overview

I*n astrology, the art of* relating events on Earth to influences in the heavens, each celestial body exerts its own form of power, which is modified according to its geometric relationship with the others. The heavens are made up of several kinds of celestial bodies. First, of course, there is the solar system—the Sun, Moon, and planets. Beyond the solar system lies the infinity of fixed stars, so-called because, as opposed to the planets, which the ancients could observe moving across the sky, the stars were always in the same place. Your horoscope plots the placement of the celestial bodies at the time of your birth.

When we speak of the heavens in astrology, we often speak of the zodiac, an imaginary belt extending nine degrees on either side of the ecliptic, the apparent path of the Sun across the sky. (Remember that the zodiac was devised in antiquity, when it was believed that the Sun revolved around the Earth.) The zodiac is divided into twelve arcs, or constellations, of thirty degrees each. Each arc is accorded a name and associated with the dates during which the Sun made its annual passage through that region of the sky at the time the zodiac was first devised. Your sun sign, the most widely known of the many astrological signs, refers to the particular arc of the zodiac through which the Sun was passing at the time of your birth. (With the procession of the equinoxes, the solar path may not always correspond to the actual solar chart.) The zodiac belt also contains the orbits of the Moon and most of the planets.

The solar system, then, constitutes the most important influence on human affairs. In ancient times, it was believed that the planets had their own light (the Sun and Moon were considered planets). Only five planets—Mercury, Venus, Mars, Jupiter, and Saturn—were visible to the ancients; Uranus, Neptune, and Pluto have been discovered over the last two hundred years. The influence of each planet depends on its position in the zodiac and its relation to the other celestial bodies, including the fixed stars. While some astrologers maintain that the planets are primarily refractors of influences from the more distant stars, most believe that each planet, along with the Sun and Moon, has its own characteristics that uniquely influence us—how we think, feel, and act. This influence can be positive and constructive or negative and self-destructive. Ultimately, the planets' disposition in your chart is a way of expressing various possibilities, which you can interpret and act upon as you choose.

The Solar System

Most astrologers agree that the primary

influences come from within our own solar system—the Sun, Moon, and planets. Each planet is said to rule over one or two signs of the zodiac and have sway over a particular part of the body. Over the centuries, each planet has come to represent or influence a different aspect of the personality.

The Sun, which rules Leo, represents the conscious, creative aspects of the self. In a chart, a well-placed, strong

Sun indicates a dignified, self-possessed, affectionate, and authoritative personality; a badly placed Sun can suggest an ostentatious and dictatorial nature. The Sun rules the heart. Solar types tend to be energetic (the Sun, after all, is our source of energy) and like to take on large-scale projects that make good use of their many talents. They often make excellent top-level executives.

On the other hand, the Moon,

which rules over zodiacal Cancer, represents the imagination and is often linked by astrologers with the unconscious, hidden part of humans. In a chart, a prominent Moon usually indicates a sensitive and vulnerable nature, which can often be quite delightful; a badly placed Moon, however, can suggest an unhealthy and even dangerous self-absorption. In terms of the body, the Moon rules over the breasts. Lunarians are adaptable and often protective; perfectly capable of enjoying the delights of a quiet life at home, many also seek the public spotlight.

Mercury, the smallest planet and the one closest to the Sun, rules Gemini and Virgo. Like the Roman messenger of the gods whose name it shares, Mercury represents communication, speech, and wit, along with an often changeable disposition. Mercurians tend to be sensitive to their environment; they epitomize verbal and written expression and are often journalists and writers.

Venus, the most brilliant planet, rules Taurus and Libra; the planet of love, it governs the higher emotions, physical beauty, creativity, sex appeal, and sensual experience in all its many forms. It has rule over the throat. Venusians love beauty and art; they can at times be concerned with the surface of things, allowing image to become everything.

Mars, the planet that physically most resembles Earth, rules over Aries; representing the physical side of life, it combines with Venus to influence our sex drive. In a chart, Mars means courage, confidence, and the aggressive urges—the result-oriented ability to take on a project and get it done. In terms of the body, Mars has sway over the sex organs, particularly for men.

Jupiter, the largest planet in the solar

system, rules Sagittarius and represents the more profound realms of thinking and mental life, as well as the depths of the spirit. Jupiter suggests generosity, loyalty, success, and steady, solid growth. In terms of the body, it has sway over the thighs, liver, and blood. Jupiterians tend to be thoughtful, even philosophical, with plenty of social skills and an adventurous love of travel; Jupiter women are often strikingly beautiful.

Saturn, the farthest from Earth of the traditional planets, represents fears, uncertainties, and materialistic concerns. It can indicate practicality, patience, and honesty, although, if badly placed in a chart, Saturn can also suggest a deep fear of life. It governs the human skeleton, emphasizing this planet's role in providing structure and control; Saturnians tend to make good accountants and bureaucrats.

Uranus, discovered in the eighteenth century, rules Aquarius. Often representing change, even upheaval, it can be a beneficent influence, representing the kind of brilliant flash of insight that can instigate bold new ways of thinking. Yet its independent and rebellious nature can pose problems, when liberty turns to license and at times even to crime.

Neptune, discovered in the mid-nineteenth century, has rule over Pisces.

On its beneficent side, it can represent idealism, art, and imagination; its connection with the sea (Neptune was the Roman god of the ocean) indicates its tendency to affect the unconscious aspects of the psyche. This can bring great power; it can also, however, suggest a preference to dream rather than act.

Pluto, discovered in 1930, now rules Scorpio. The planet farthest from the Sun, Pluto often represents the dark

forces of desire and instinct that seek
dissolution of the self within the great
cosmos. While there are dangers here,
there is as well the potential for profound
healing.

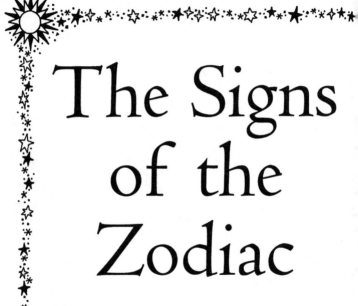

The Signs
of the
Zodiac

When we speak of the signs of the zodiac,

we refer to the twelve thirty-degree arcs of the sky into which the zodiac is divided. Each sign is represented by an image derived from ancient descriptions of the constellations; however, the astrological signs of the zodiac should not be confused with the actual constellations whose names they sometimes share. The most important signs are the sun signs, by which is meant the particular zone of the sky through which the Sun was passing at the time of someone's birth.

The signs of the zodiac are as follows:

Aries (the Ram), March 21–April 20

Taurus (the Bull), April 21–May 21

Gemini (the Twins), May 22–June 21

Cancer (the Crab), June 22–July 23

Leo (the Lion), July 24–August 23

Virgo (the Virgin), August 24–September 23

Libra (the Scales), September 24–October 23

Scorpio (the Scorpion), October 24–November 22

Sagittarius (the Archer), November 23–December 21

Capricorn (the Goat), December 22–January 20

Aquarius (the Water Bearer), January 21–February 19

Pisces (the Fish), February 20–March 20

The zodiacal signs are also symbols for the great forces that lie deeply within our minds, hearts, and souls and exist in different combinations from one person to the next. Each sign is associated with a different part of the body. In total, the twelve signs express all that we are as hu-

mans. The signs are said to be composed
of four different elements and three different qualities.

55

The Four
Elements

The *four elements* through which the twelve signs of the zodiac are expressed are fire, earth, air, and water. For the Greeks, they were the fundamental substances of the universe. In astrology, these elements are also spiritual and symbolic; they are expressed in connection with three different qualities—cardinal, fixed, and mutable. Each element has one cardinal sign, one fixed sign, and one mutable sign; and each quality is expressed through each element, as in the chart that follows:

	Cardinal	*Fixed*	*Mutable*
Fire	Aries	Leo	Sagittarius
Earth	Capricorn	Taurus	Virgo
Air	Libra	Aquarius	Gemini
Water	Cancer	Scorpio	Pisces

In addition, the four elements, which are restless and in conflict with one another, are often said to be bound together by a mysterious, invisible fifth element, known as the "quintessence," which is responsible for maintaining the often tenuous unity of all things on Earth.

Fire Signs

*T*he fire element, expressed through Aries, Leo, and Sagittarius, is profoundly linked to the spirit. Fire is a powerful elemental force; impulsive, iconoclastic, and warm, the fire signs are eternally seeking expression. If not regulated in some way, however, fire can turn destructive, burning out of control.

Aries—outgoing, idealistic, enthusiastic—requires great freedom in order to achieve its maximum sense of self. Often brimming with confidence, the Aries type tends to act impulsively and not always with proper concern for what other people may think or feel. This spontaneity can be tremendously attractive, but it can at times become selfish and over-bearing.

Leo, on the other hand, while also possessing a deep need for freedom, tends to be much more sensitive to others. Given to the exuberant and flamboyant, Leo's creativity is frequently expressed through art and drama. Self-reliant and generally optimistic, the Leo nature also has a vein of altruism; Leos can, though, at times be a bit vain.

Sagittarius, the mutable fire sign, is characterized by qualities of profound yearning and aspiration. Open, honest, and generous, Sagittarians tend to be hungry for growth and expansion. They are very independent—sometimes to a fault—and are often great seekers, for whom the journey is more important than the destination.

Earth Signs

*T*he earth element, expressed through Taurus, Virgo, and Capricorn, is deeply connected to physical things. Generally, it reflects the practical, down-to-earth side of human nature. It is also said to be an incarnating principle by which spirituality takes on form. Not surprisingly, the earth and water elements enjoy a close relationship, with earth stabilizing water and water making the arid earth fertile.

Taurus, the fixed earth sign, tends toward the sedentary. Slow, practical, and conservative, a person born under Taurus will likely evidence an unspectacular, solid determination. Taurus is receptive to the joys of a gentle, stable existence—a regular paycheck, a nice house, warm relationships, a comfortable routine. When frustrated or threatened, however, the Taurus nature can turn possessive and jealous.

Virgo, the mutable earth element, is drawn toward ephemeral things, engrossed in "what is past, or passing, or to come." Intellectual, elegant, intelligent, and methodical, Virgo is driven to seek the clarity of understanding. When subjected to intense stress, though, Virgo can become hypercritical and a bit of a nag.

Capricorn, the cardinal earth element, is dependable, solid, trustworthy, and prudent. The Capricorn nature will plow steadily ahead, connected to its roots and clear about what it wishes to achieve in life. Yet in stressful situations Capricorn can become selfish and rigid.

Air Signs

*T*he air element, expressed through Gemini, Libra, and Aquarius, has long been associated with thought, dating back to the ancient concept that thinking is the process by which humans take in ideas from the world around them, much as they take in air through breathing. All three air signs generally are dominated by tendencies toward restlessness; they are also known as the nervous signs. However, they are each unique.

Gemini is particularly volatile, a whirlwind constantly blowing in many directions. The Gemini nature is inventive, alert, and communicative, but Geminis

can at times become unstable and wild,
even hysterical.

Libra is like a strong wind that
blows purposefully in a single direction.
Its influence is elegant and orderly. Li-
bras tend to be perceptive and affectionate, sensitive to others and aware of their
needs, although in excess a Libra nature
can be impractical and a bit lazy.

Aquarius, the calmest air sign, is associated with water as well as air; it rep-

resents spiritual knowledge, creativity, and freedom. The Aquarian nature tends toward the rational and places great value on freedom, sometimes sacrificing the future in the name of rebellion.

Water Signs

The water element, expressed through Cancer, Pisces and Scorpio, represents the fluidity, spirituality, and sensitivity in our nature. Often emotional, sometimes to the point of instability, the water element needs to find some kind of container in order to realize its true potential.

Cancer, represented by the Crab, is emotional, imaginative, and romantic; it can also be very cautious. There is something gentle and shy about the Cancer nature; afraid of being hurt, it is sometimes slow to come out of—and quick to return to—its shell. Such vulnerability can be deeply touching; in excess, however, it can turn moody and self-absorbed.

Scorpio, the most self-confident of the water signs, is masterful, shrewd, and determined. Possessed of strong desires, Scorpio types are not easily dissuaded from pursuing their goals. In doing so, they can be forceful and inspirational; yet when threatened, they can exhibit a violent streak, and when thwarted they can turn sarcastic and cruel.

Emotional and highly intuitive Pisces is also quick to retreat from the slings and arrows of life. Often this is because the Pisces nature is so sensitive to the emotional needs of others that it will sometimes forget its own interests and need to seek temporary refuge, in order to find its own center again. It has to be careful, though, not to fall into the trap of self-pity.

The Three Qualities

T<i>here are three quali-</i>ties, or modes of expression, through which each of the four elements finds expression in the twelve signs of the zodiac: cardinality, fixity, and mutability.

The qualities are another way of expressing features the different signs share; all
four fixed signs, for example, will have certain features in common, in that they will
tend to be more stable than the mutable
signs within their same element. This may
seem complicated, but the basic principle
is actually pretty simple.

The cardinal quality serves as the
origin of action, the wellspring of energy
that gets things done in the world. It's the

"mover and shaker" personality—active, outward-looking, more geared to "doing" than to "being." The four cardinal signs are Aries, Cancer, Libra, and Capricorn; each is self-assertive, but in a unique way. Capricorn, the earth cardinal sign, tends to take solid, dependable action that is often geared toward material success, while Aries, the fire sign, often acts in a much more spontaneous, even impulsive, way. Libra, the air sign, is particularly assertive on the intellectual level, quick to advance its ideas and defend them when they are questioned. Cancer, the water sign, tends toward caution and often will act prudently.

The fixed quality serves to temper movement; it functions as an impediment, an often valuable check on the rampant free flow of energy. Sometimes expressed as "will," the fixed signs—Taurus, Leo, Scorpio, and Aquarius—are likely to be resistant to change and appreciate tradition and known, sure values. Taurus, the earth sign, is the most sedentary of all, with deep, latent powers and a clear preference for staying in one place. Leo, the fire sign, embodies a sustained emotional warmth and loyalty that is not likely to change over time. With Scorpio, the water sign, power takes on a more fluid form, exhibiting an unshakable self-confidence that remains firm in the face of adversity. Aquarius, meanwhile, is the most cool and composed of the air signs; Aquarians trust rational thinking and extend deep roots into the ideas they hold and the places where they live.

The mutable quality embodies the principles of flexibility and adaptability. The mutable signs—Gemini, Virgo, Sagittarius, and Pisces—could be said to combine aspects of cardinal impulsiveness with those of the unyielding fixed temperament. Gemini, the mutable air sign, is particularly given to surprising transformations of the self; you think you know a Gemini, and then, *presto!* you realize that you knew only one side of the person's nature. Virgo, the earth sign, is often irresistibly drawn toward the shifting play of ideas and thought. For Sagittarius, the fire sign, change often equals growth; driven to expand, the Sagittarian nature seems eternally questing after something new. Pisces, the water sign, often embodies the fluid, changing character of the emotions; sensitive to the smallest alterations of feelings, it can ride the waves of emotional life like a skilled surfer.

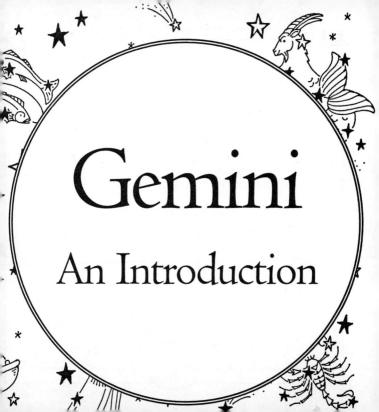

Gemini

An Introduction

Thismutable air sign is the most versatile, magnetic, clever, and communicative member of the zodiac—so much so, indeed, that you require two people, the Twins, as a symbol. Your intelligence, creativity, and inventiveness can hardly be equaled; and although it may seem as if everything you do is methodically thought out and planned, you act, more often than not, on the spur of the inspired moment.

Because of your tireless wit, original style, and variety of talents, you will be constantly enlisted to keep people entertained; and if you occasionally feel abused by all this, you must keep in mind that you rarely expose your serious side even to your friends. They cannot help thinking of you as the life of the party. If you ever grow weary of this role, you will discover that people like you anyway.

Youthful good looks, childlike naïveté, and irrepressible charm are your birthright, but you tend to be more interested in surfaces than in depths. You are a brilliant conversationalist, for example, who can discourse fluently on almost any subject under the sun, but you will falter, or even fall silent, when confronting serious emotions. You would rather take in an engrossing film with a plot you can discuss for hours on end than share your intimate feelings even with those you love. These ambiguities are perfectly captured by the mysterious Gemini glyph, which can be viewed as the Roman numeral two, a set of pillars, or even parallel lines representing the contrasting, though not necessarily contradictory, personalities of the Twins.

Myths
and
Legends

We adore enchant-
ing tales of dwarfs, giants,

radiant maidens, and knights in shining armor, of glittering heroes and impossibly black-hearted villains, but classical mythology is also filled with darker, more brooding stories in which right and wrong are muddied, and justice doesn't always prevail. Heroes are sometimes cripplingly, even fatally, flawed; siblings are either wholly devoted to each other's happiness or fanatically committed to destruction. The two great myths associated with Twins are an important part of this murky heritage.

According to Roman legend, Mars, the god of war, raped a vestal virgin; Romulus and Remus were the result. They were set adrift on the Tiber but rescued and nurtured by a she-wolf; eventually they were discovered by a shepherd. Years later, as the twins were mapping out a new city, they fell into a heated argument; Romulus killed Remus and established the seat of Rome. He himself committed a series of rapes against the Sabine women and died under mysterious circumstances.

The Greek twins, Castor and Pollux, have a less troubled, though equally complicated, history. The story begins with Leda, whose husband was king Tyndareus of Sparta; their union gave rise to Castor. At the same time, however, Leda was also raped by Zeus, the king of the gods, who disguised himself as a swan, and thus was Pollux born. Two boys, one mortal, the other divine—but these twins were inseparable.

The godly Pollux was a boxer; his agility and speed are associated with Gemini. The mortal Castor became a great horseman and charioteer; these are symbols of Sagittarius, which is Gemini's polar opposite. In a bitter dispute with a rival cattle owner, Castor was murdered;

and although Pollux in turn killed the man responsible, his grief knew no bounds. Not all the vengeance in the world could revive his beloved twin, and Pollux remained devastated and inconsolable. He even begged his father to let him die so that he could join his brother in Heaven.

Castor wasn't a god, so the crafty Zeus suggested a bargain wherein the brothers could reside together throughout eternity—half the year in the under-world and the other half in Heaven. During the latter sojourn, their twin stars can be observed in the magnificent night sky—the two most luminous bodies in the constellation of Gemini.

Symbols
and
Associations

The earliest hiero-
glyphics and pictographs

appeared in China and Egypt during the age of Gemini (6000–4000 B.C.), when disparate cultures began trading. The invention of the wheel expedited commerce and furthered communication among these agricultural communities, and a twin set of pillars, representing gods, often stood at the gates of ancient temples, which they were said to protect.

Every zodiacal sign has a ruling planet and a detrimental planet, which are strengthened and weakened respectively when placed in that particular sign. Mercury (named for the Greco-Roman messenger of the gods) rules Gemini, supplying dexterity, speed, quick-wittedness, and ease of communication, but Jupiter, the planet of expansion, is detrimental, or not very comfortable, there.

Geminis are *versatile, charming, adaptable, flexible, youthful, intelligent, rational, ingenious, inquisitive, witty, objective, independent.* You net-

work effectively, have cheerful disposi-
tions, and possess superb gifts for getting
your messages across.

Twins can also be *two-sided, inconsistent, detached, irresponsible, childish, changeable,
nervous, restless, mischievous, coy, excitable, frivo-
lous, gossipy,* and *superficial.* You are emotionally shallow and spread yourselves
too thin.

Gemini archetypes are the clown,
magician, alchemist, artist, inventor, and

eternal youth. Professions include jour-
nalist, writer, musician, mime, juggler,
comedian, teacher, translator, linguist,
lecturer, marketing executive, advertising
executive, public relations specialist, sec-
retary, travel agent, and salesman.

Parts of the body ruled by the Twins
include the shoulders, arms, hands, and
lungs; Mercury governs the nervous and
respiratory systems. Gemini countries include Belgium and Wales. London, Mel-

bourne, San Francisco, Versailles, and Nuremberg are Gemini cities.

Colors associated with Gemini are yellow and orange. If you were born between May 22 and May 31, your birthstone is emerald. If you were born between June 1 and June 21, your birthstone is pearl. Other gems associated with Gemini are agate, beryl, opal, and tiger's eye. Gemini's metal is mercury, also known as quicksilver.

Plants ruled by Gemini include branches, grass, underbrush, yarrow, and woodbine. Flowers are dandelion and lily of the valley. Gemini foods include red beets, lemon, celery, grapefruit, parsnip, wheat, cauliflower, orange, asparagus, and tomato. Herbs and spices are comfrey, marigold, vervain, and licorice.

Famous Gemini personalities include F. Lee Bailey, Barbara Bush, George Bush, Joan Collins, Judy Garland, Michael J.

Fox, Newt Gingrich, Steffi Graf, John Fitzgerald Kennedy, Henry Kissinger, Paul McCartney, Marilyn Monroe, Bill Moyers, Prince Philip of England, The Artist Formerly Known As Prince, Isabella Rosellini, and Peter Yarrow.

The Gemini motto is "I think, therefore I am."

Health
and
Physique

The Gemini type is frequently distinguished

by a long, thin face, arched eyebrows, high cheekbones, angular nose, and pointed chin. You are usually medium to tall in height, and lanky or average in weight; and your expressive body language—roving eyes, flailing arms, inveterate pacing back and forth—immediately sets you apart from other zodiacal signs.

The nervous temperament, quick metabolism, and (in extreme cases) overactive thyroid that typify your sign will allow you to burn calories effortlessly: Twins need never worry about gaining unwanted pounds. Indeed, you will often be so preoccupied with intellectual pursuits that you may forget the daily niceties of taking care of yourself—like sitting down to a proper meal. From time to time, you may even be tempted to survive on nicotine, caffeine, or other stimulants. In the long run, however, this will deplete your energy rather than increase it.

Every zodiacal sign corresponds to a part of the human anatomy, so the horoscope can reveal which organs and areas of the body may be vulnerable and prone to illness. Gemini rules the hands, so computers may begin to occupy a great deal of your time; and once you pull onto the information superhighway, you will be addicted for life. But endless hours word processing or surfing the net can result in hunched shoulders, bad posture, or carpal tunnel syndrome, so be sure to find a very comfortable chair and take hourly breaks.

Air signs require constant mental stimulation, so you may become exceedingly irritable if your mind is not occupied with inventive ideas and visionary schemes. If you persist in exerting yourself mentally while remaining physically inactive, however, you may wind up with eyestrain, headaches, and even migraines. In addition, because Gemini rules the lungs and respiratory system, you may have a tendency toward bronchitis, chest colds, asthma, or even, at the extreme, pneumonia and emphysema; and in stressful situations, you may start hyperventilating or have trouble catching your breath. To ward off such ills, you would be well-advised to practice deep-breathing exercises, yoga, biofeedback, or related relaxation techniques.

Exercise can also relieve stress, but don't overdo it at first. Since you love to think on your feet, try reading some classical philosophy while on the stationary bike or StairMaster. Or tune in to books on tape while you stroll through the neighborhood park. You'll be healthy *and* well-read!

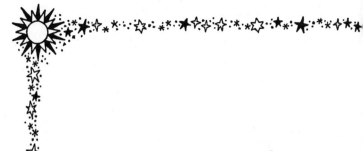

Personality

I*n certain ways your twin tendencies simply*

divide, and you are brilliant, talkative, witty, but also inconsistent, unreliable, and irredeemably sarcastic. In other ways they come together to make you the eternal chameleon: flexible, capable, and always willing to adjust to any set of circumstances, lightning quick, and able either to dart away from danger or to blend in seamlessly with your surroundings. If you are ever stuck, or your professional circumstances seem stagnant, you won't hesitate to make a switch; but then you also might simply decide to relieve the boredom by taking up another project alongside the first ... or dropping the first one altogether. Variety is the spice of life to you, and you love few things more than juggling two or three activities at once: feeding the kids, typing a report for work, and making plane reservations to Rio. After that, you might solve a math problem or two.

As the most mobile sign of the zodiac, you must be constantly bombarded by stimuli, or you will leave and go somewhere else; and although this does not mean that you can never hold down a permanent job or carry on a long-term relationship, it will create certain problems. You are a fascinating dinner companion and raconteur, for example, but you tend to overload your schedule to the point where you are frequently expected to be in two places at once. Then you will be late or have to cancel an engagement, and even your closest friends will be exasperated by your overwhelming (and consistent) chaos. They will also wonder how in the world they can still like you so much. But they do.

And why? Because, for all of your faults and your irritating behavior, for all of your cavalier assumption that you can get away with anything, you are still the most charming and exciting person around, and you can always be relied upon to make people laugh. Once every other avenue has been exhausted, you will manage to come up with something crazy and inventive. No one can stay mad at you for long, therefore, and life would unquestionably be duller without you.

Still, you should not rely too much upon your vivacity, because the annoyances you cause are not *always* minor—

and charm is not a license for boorishness. Don't discover this too late. Otherwise, your friends may not be too eager to be in your company.

Career

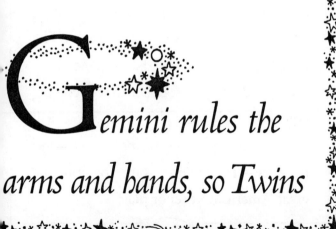

Gemini rules the arms and hands, so Twins

make excellent computer operators, word processors, secretaries, and journalists. In addition, your sign is marked by cleverness and speed, so you also excel at writing songs, slogans, and advertising jingles. The long haul, on the other hand, is not your forte, so despite your talent for concocting ever-more-elaborate plot twists, you will have to develop more staying power—and patience— if you ever want to write the great American novel or play.

Exceptional timing and rhythm provide you with a fine ear for music; you are especially adroit with percussion instruments, which require highly nimble fingers. The same timing, along with your fluent speaking skills and ready wit, could also incline you to comedy, whether it be slapstick or stand-up. Dexterity and speed make you adept at running, fencing, boxing, dancing, pantomime, clowning, or any other activity in which being quick on your feet makes all the difference; and even when these activities do not define your professional goals, one or more of them will almost certainly become a serious and passionate pastime.

All of these talents will make you highly valuable. Add to them your quicksilver adaptability, fast responses, and ever-ready invention, and you will find yourself splendidly positioned to market any product you choose, including the most important commodity of all: you. Merchandising, public relations, advertising, and sales will call upon all of your charm and communication prowess, indeed, and will make you feel very much at home. Your poker face would make you handy at delivering the news; or, in a slightly different vein and if you are so inclined, you might become a wonderful used car salesman, con artist, or swindler! An inordinate number of politicians are born under the sign of Gemini.

In the end, you will excel in any field that requires—and rewards—intelligence, flexibility, and a talent for getting the job done quickly and efficiently. You are also gratified when people seek (and even more when they follow) your advice, so you will be very attracted to fields like teaching, lecturing, counseling, and even astrology. These professions will draw on your unique ability to analyze and communicate your conclusions in a manner that is at once lucid, emotionally detached, yet highly compassionate. And that, for you, is the ultimate gift.

Love
and
Marriage

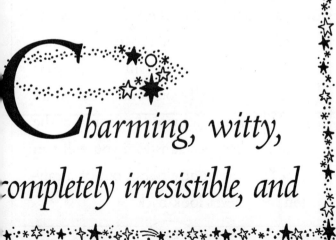

Charming, witty,

completely irresistible, and

not a little conceited, you have always been thoroughly aware of the mesmerizing effect you have on everyone you meet. Anyone who makes the hideous mistake of trying to go beyond the trance to draw close to you, however, will destroy your peace of mind. If you could, you would wave your magic wand and make the intruder disappear. Instead, you will run away (or have yourself shot out of a cannon) and never look back.

You were dripping with friendliness and invitation at your first meeting— indeed, you were the best of friends— but the minute your relationship moves from the platonic to the romantic plane, you will be as cold and insensitive as an iceberg. Suddenly, without warning, as quickly as you have professed your undying love, you will realize that you are in over your head and break off the romance with a snap of your agile fin-

135

gers. And why? Because you want to put off marriage as long as you can—forever, if that's possible—so the faintest hint of a question about what you may be doing a week from now will set off alarms. Even your friends may hold you in contempt for this.

And yet, for all of your talk about dodging the bullets of love and romance, you seem never to be without someone draped over your shoulder. As far as you are concerned, being alone in the dark with no one to turn on the light could be a fate even worse than a long-term commitment, so you may go through numerous relationships, even life-changing ones, before you finally take that terrifying plunge into permanence.

And when you do, you will lose none of your excitement and fire. It's not for you to stay at home cooking and cleaning and watching TV. You will want to be out on the town and kicking up your heels . . . unless you can find your perfect partner, one who wildly titillates your mind. With such a treasure at home, you will feel less and less desire to stray. You are also the perennial student, so if your loved one can teach you a few things you don't already know about the facts of life, you will be a willing and eager prisoner for years to come.

Home
and
Family

E

ven as your friends

succumb one by one to the

finality of settling down, you will still dream of staying up late and having a ball. But with whom? All your old pals are tied up. And is tea for two really as terrifying as all that?

No; and once you explore it seriously, you may even decide that intimate conversation with someone you love can be infinitely more gratifying than the superficial chatter you have always been used to. Even then, however, it will still be true that spending more time at home will be a lot easier for you if the home entertainment center is well-stocked with a video library, CDs, and a variety of books to keep your mind occupied.

When you are not on the sofa, absorbed by the television, you will probably be holed up in your home office, hypnotized by the smaller, yet no less enticing, computer screen; and once that happens, your airy life will *really* change.

You may forget to eat; you may forget to leave your little den altogether. If some poor soul is trying to hook you, he or she need do nothing more than outfit the house with the proper equipment, and plenty of it. You may never leave your castle again. Of course, even with all those expensive gadgets around, you still love chatting with your mate into the wee hours of the night.

Because you have always felt unprepared for parenthood, you may delay having children; yet once you pass the initial stages of extreme self-doubt and decide to go ahead (and once the kids stop waking you up in the middle of the night), the most amazing transformation will take place. You, a childlike Gemini, will immerse yourself resoundingly in the realm of make-believe and have a captive audience to boot; and suddenly the world will discover that no one is better suited, or better able, to hang out with children than you, who once had been so full of fears. You will be surprised at how much you love reading to your children and putting on plays with them. Escorting them to museums and the circus may bring back memories of your own youth . . . but be sure they are fast asleep when you stay up past midnight watching old movies, or you may raise a brood of couch potatoes.

Think again before convincing yourself unequivocally that marriage and children will tie you down. In fact, they will
keep you eternally young. You will certainly consider that well worth the wait.

Gemini
in Love

I f you can't be with the one you love, honey, love the one you're with." This refrain perfectly describes your attitude toward love and romance: chilled, cavalier, and matter-of-fact. Although love is not friendship, nor friendship love, the two may become confused in your perpetually indecisive mind, and often the only attitude you can take toward romantic passion is one of unabashed detachment, not because you are necessarily lacking in ardor, but rather because you are often of two (Twin) minds on the all-important subject of commitment. It usually proves far less taxing to like than to love.

Just when the fires begin to burn the brightest, you will begin to wonder if the glow mightn't be rosier over there, or over *there*—anywhere, in fact, but the place you currently occupy. It isn't; you simply do not want to feel the heat that threatens. Talking yourself out of it will do you no good because other fires will start, so you might as well plunge in.

It should be easy enough to know the real thing, because your truest love is one you can trust wholeheartedly. When you finally take those scary vows, you want to make sure you do so with a friend of the highest order who will understand your every thought, whether you utter it or not. Once you stop erecting artificial distinctions between friendship and love, you may finally break down the barriers to your heart. And once *those* floodgates open, there will be no turning back.

Gemini with Aries

MARCH 21–APRIL 20

Aries is impulsive, independent, and frequently unreliable: in your life one minute and out the door the next. If you embark on a relationship with this cardinal fire sign ruled by dynamic Mars, you may be reminded, a trifle uncomfortably, of yourself—especially that part of you that finds it difficult to stay at home and lead a quiet life. These two airplanes will pass in the night—at six hundred miles an hour!

If you could spend your ideal day doing *anything* you liked, you might begin with numerous cups of coffee strong enough to melt the spoons. Cordless phone (your most prized possession) propped comfortably on your shoulder, you would then catch up on all the gossip with various friends while simultaneously reading the paper, ironing your clothes, and perhaps paying the bills. Finally, you make it out the door in a flash before realizing you forgot to eat breakfast, but you can worry about that later. Just as you are locking up, your fiery favorite, Aries, returns, breathless but invigorated after an early-morning run. You hadn't even realized the Ram was gone. A brief peck on the cheek, a briefer dash to your car, and then a busy several hours of shopping, museums, lunch with a friend, a movie, more shopping, coffee with another pal, and a video to rent on your way home.

And the Ram? Up at the crack of dawn, bolt out the door, run around the track, gobble down some food, help friends lay down a new carpet, lunch, tennis, and so on until well past the dinner hour. The activities may be very different—indeed, fundamentally divergent—but the patterns are the same, and each of you respects the other's freedom so much that you may never spend time as a couple. And, chances are, the two of you will be so busy with your separate lives that you may not even notice that you haven't spent much time together.

At least you will not grow bored, but will you actually have a life that you can share? And if you are never together, how can you build trust? You are two of the most restless signs in the zodiac, so if you have a quarrel, you will both take cover somewhere else. Of course you two will probably be too busy to fight, but when you do have a tiff, neither one of you will be the first to resolve it.

The only solution may be to think

of this relationship as a balancing act. If you can stop the Ram's running around long enough to introduce it to the wondrous world of the intellect, and Aries can cool off your ceaseless intellection long enough for you to feel the earth beneath your feet again, then you might have a foundation on which to build. Take the Ram to your favorite art gallery one weekend, and let the Ram take you on a long hike. Otherwise, your only common bond may be the time you spend apart.

You might also sign a pact agreeing to meet at the end of the day no matter what you have been doing, because that will make your nights worth coming home to. You are full of imagination in the bedroom; the Ram is full of fire. Your combustions can bring endless hours of pleasure to you both; and once *those* two airplanes meet, you will certainly want to do so more often. Then you may even decide that, for all of your roaming, there is, indeed, no place like home.

Gemini with Taurus

APRIL 21–MAY 21

You *are flighty, high-*strung, and unable to make plans more than a day in advance. Taurus is slow, patient, responsible, and the acme of stability. A relationship with this fixed earth sign will bring you down to earth and closer to home; and the Bull's smoldering sensuality (which it inherits from Venus, the goddess of love) should give you good—indeed excellent—reason for staying there.

What will Taurus receive in return? Excitement. Don't let the surface fool you: Although the Bull may appear to be (and indeed often is) perfectly content, it secretly longs for someone to pull it out of its habitual rut. Boredom is your mortal enemy, so you will arrive like a breath of fresh air on the Taurean doorstep; and just when the Bull is moaning that it will never be able to shake its routine, you will pull a trick out of your sleeve and change night to day; you will become the life of the party and help the Bull kick up its hooves. Just remember one thing: Flirting, to you, is harmless, and as natural as breathing, but to jealous Taurus it is a mortal sin. This sign wrestles with insecurity every day, so don't give it fuel, and do not take the Bull for granted. If you do, Taurus will throw its weight around; and then you, in terror, will be out the door.

So what are the odds that this union will last longer than the nanoseconds of your own attention span? Better than you might think; in many ways you are the answers to each other's prayers. Taurus can sit still for hours staring into your eyes; you start to fidget if a minute goes by without some action. Imbibe just a little of that Taurean calm, and your life could benefit appreciably. You can skip meals and never even notice; the Bull can gorge itself with equal senselessness. Your restlessness and activity could help melt those unwanted calories away—and that would be a Taurean dream come true.

You will constantly drag the sluggish Bull out of the house; the Bull will always make sure that you find your way home. You can burn yourself out with too little sleep; Taurus will see that you get all the rest you need. Eating and sleeping are as important to the Bull as thinking and talking are to you, so both of you will draw on each other's strengths and help minimize each other's weaknesses. Nor will you feel that you are being cheated in any way of your disco nights and other enjoyments, because Taurus is one of the most sensual members of the zodiac. Taurus will entertain you at home—by creating lavish, delicious meals for you. The Bull may start to yawn and turn into a pumpkin as midnight rolls around, but toddle through the bedroom door and it will suddenly find a second wind—and perhaps a third. You will certainly have nothing to complain about on that score.

Spend a night in the Bull's domain and you will finally understand what you never could before: that silence can indeed be golden.

Gemini with Gemini

MAY 22–JUNE 21

Your planetary ruler has bestowed upon you the gift of eternal youth—not through a magical elixir or a secret club but through the happenstance of your own nature. You, by a fortunate twist of fate, always appear younger than you actually are and teem with an energy unequaled in the zodiac, so if you embark on a relationship with another mutable air sign, neither will ever have to worry that one is aging better than the other. If this seems shallow, it is; and before you start planning the rest of your lives together, you should be aware of other drawbacks.

You have never seen yourself as others see you: fidgety, nervous, incapable of standing still. Now you will have your chance; now you will try to gaze into eyes that flick restlessly, relentlessly around the room and seem to light everywhere except on your own. Now you will thrill—in the beginning—to see another brilliant mind at work; then you will be driven mad by all that incessant talking and grow furious at the way your Twin can jabber away for hours without paying the slightest attention to anything you say.

On the other hand, you will have a very trusting companion in a second Gemini, and no other zodiacal sign places so high a premium on friendship. You will constantly go to the movies, share new ideas, ruminate about everything under the sun; you may even explore the exciting new world of cyberspace, which is only a push button away. Just be sure to get two computers, and make every effort to come down to earth—at least once in a while. You have been searching for your lost Twin throughout your life. Now you may have found it.

But be advised that, although a legendary friendship may grow, a romantic union might fizzle. As much as you enjoy the same activities and can swear eternal allegiance, you will both put your emotions on the back burner—by choice.

And whereas this might be the very thing for platonic friendships, it could be the kiss of death to any sort of passionate union. On the other hand, if you can both sit still long enough to look each other in the eyes and put your nimble minds to intelligent use, you should be able to overcome any difficulty—if you want to. But that is the rub.

Pairing with your restless and will-o'-the-wisp Twin could prove to be the greatest challenge of your life. It could also become your deepest satisfaction. Your mystery and mutability may be vexing for others who never quite know what you are thinking from moment to moment or what you will do next, but they may be exactly the alchemical ingredients you need for an intense and lasting relationship. Indeed, you may eschew commitment entirely, which would be impossible for most other signs: That touch of intrigue, that doubt about whether or not it might all end tomorrow, or even today, could keep you fascinated for years to come—or for as long as it lasts.

Gemini with Cancer

Secretive, emotional, and
highly protective of family and friends,
the Crab is one of the zodiac's great enig-
mas. You, with your restless intelligence,

love nothing more than a puzzle against which you can pit all of your energy and wit; and even after you've settled into a long-term relationship with this cardinal water sign, you will still feel as if each day presents a new mystery to be solved.

Just be sure that your unrelenting curiosity to know *everything* doesn't kill this relationship altogether. Cancer is the most private sign of the zodiac; if you probe and pry and insist on revealing its secrets before it is ready, you may send the Crab scurrying straight back into its shell and only see its snapping pincers from then on. Talk to the Crab, nurture the Crab, help the Crab through its wayward emotional shifts, but do not badger or interrogate or indulge in sarcasm—or mind games. Be gentle and supportive for a change; once you melt that Cancerian heart, it will be yours for keeps.

Getting there will be the problem

because the wary and intuitive Crab will initially distrust this restless and fast-talking Gemini; and despite its own problems opening up to people, Cancer admires candor. You will have to convince the Crab that, although you may use clever aphorisms to elude confrontation, you are not necessarily deceptive, dishonest, or coy. (The alternative, however—admitting that you are avoiding your heart—will not score many points.)

And although you may not mean to hurt this crustacean with your sardonic manner, you have no idea how acerbic your barbs can be—or how painfully the ultra-sensitive Crab recoils from them. Words are your weapons, but to Cancer they are poisonous darts. Shoot too many into that soft and yielding flesh, and your romance will be at a permanent end.

The Crab's tough outer shell is misleading because underneath, it is as vulnerable as a kitten in a dog pound. Hurts and insults do not bounce off Cancer's back: They fester. And in the end they will bring out the Crab's secret weapon, which may prove even deadlier than your own: utter and absolute silence, disappearance, withdrawal into the deep. This can tear you to pieces because you abhor a void, and without an attentive listener eagerly awaiting your every word, what will you do? You may start getting the bends. Unless you become a kinder, gentler Gemini, this Crab will scuttle out of your life and never return.

So is there hope for a duo with such drastically different outlooks and emotional makeups? Cancer's ferocious jealousy will quickly pall; your easy flirtatiousness will only stoke that bitterness the more. You like to be footloose and fancy-free; the Crab is inclined to smother. How can you possibly come together? In the bedroom—there Cancer's torrential storms can lead you to heights of ecstasy you have rarely known. Only if each of you can accept that the other is a tempest (one intellectual, the other emotional) will you have a chance.

Gemini with Leo

JULY 24–AUGUST 23

L*eo is dramatic, ego-*
tistical, and self-directed, a fixed fire sign
ruled by the blistering Sun. When you two
clash, sparks will shoot into the strato-

sphere; wit, creativity, and excitement will splash all over the heavens; and every act will be an attempt at superiority, territoriality, one-upmanship on the grandest scale. The zodiac does not contain a more magnetic or attractive couple, and people will be overjoyed just to behold you. As other signs sit around moping and wondering what to do, the two of you will bounce ideas off each other like bullets. The greatest danger may be exhaustion.

Doubly inspiring is the fact that your brainstorms will yield concrete results. You often stumble over your own plethora of ideas, but Leo is the great stage manager of the zodiac and can oversee any job waiting to be done. If you ignore the Lion's bombastic antics, and Leo discards your more pretentious suggestions, the two of you could become the most prolific twosome under the sun. But pitfalls do lurk.

As the thespian of the zodiac, Leo lives in a self-created universe in which every day is a new and exciting theatrical event, and in which the Lion is always in the spotlight. Even if all the world's a stage, you may nevertheless feel as if you are a mere bit player thereon. You, normally the life of the party, are not accustomed to this role; and Leo, who normally bellows out orders and expects, imperiously, to be obeyed, is not accustomed to using tact. Even if the Lion loves you, it also loves having you around for intellectual prestige. A consummate judge of talent, Leo knows exactly what it has found in you. Your job is to shine as the Lion directs you.

If you want this relationship to last, therefore, you will have to inform Leo that you will not be a pawn in its wild and glamorous game—and that you have your own rules. The Lion will quickly recognize your versatility; it will also have to realize your threat. Leo meticulously rehearses every line of its superbly conceived scripts and does not appreciate deviations, but you have mastered the art of improvisation, and you will not hesitate to change the plot at a moment's notice and walk straight out the door. Spontaneity and change are your rules of thumb, and the more unknown the terrain, the better. Leo, on the other hand, may pretend to be open to all of life's mysteries, but this feline needs to be king of the jungle and master of its own fate at all times.

So, although this combination of air and fire promises explosions on end, you have to make sure that something other than sheer drama holds you together when the crowds disappear and the applause dies down. But necessity is the mother of invention, and when two of the most creative signs in the zodiac put their heads together, they should be able to make each other soar in ways the rest of the world could scarcely even imagine—or ever see.

Gemini with Virgo

AUGUST 24–SEPTEMBER 23

V*irgo, though high-strung,* is also sensible, modest, and prudent; yet this mutable earth sign comes under the rulership of your own Mercury. But whereas earthy, pragmatic Virgo trains its well-ordered brain to run a tight ship and store money in the bank, you often squander your gifts in sparkling yet meaningless gab, and spend money as if it were air. The Virgin ceaselessly analyzes to arrive at the truth of the matter; you can volley back and forth till you're blue in the face and still not arrive at a conclusion.

Both of you are nervous and restless,

but Virgo is shy, introspective, and be-comingly humble. Given the opportunity and desire, the Virgin could match wits with you at a finger-snap—but why bother? This sign has better things to do than generate plans without vision or end. At the same time, however, Virgo possesses an altruistic streak and might derive a certain satisfaction from taking you in hand. And because you also share a passion for the new and experimental, you will never run out of things to keep you interested, even where your interests diverge. Indeed, your very differences may set off useful sparks.

Problems may arise when the ultra-critical Virgin starts anatomizing your every fault, but you should understand that your mate is only doing it for your own good: Virgo always wants to make everything better. In any case, you will simply change the subject, and your mercurial Virgin will instantly follow your lead. Unlike you, however, Virgo has a long attention span, and however much time you may dedicate to your many diversions, eventually that relentless mind will return to its initial theme. If you know what's good for you, you'll listen, and for two reasons. One is that nothing annoys either of you more than speaking without being listened to. The other is that Virgo is frequently right.

If the complaint is about your care-lessness, for example, you should try to use your inventive brain to find a compromise. If not, your tendency to scatter your possessions everywhere, and Virgo's desire to clean up and discard constantly (or, on a larger scale, your penchant for sweeping beginnings with no follow-through, and Virgo's need to dot every *i*), will be an ongoing argument with no end in sight. Neither of you can or will change your habits, so is there any hope for this tempestuous duo?

Yes. Business wheeling and dealing fascinates you, so if you continue to generate new ideas at a breakneck pace, and Virgo keeps meticulous files, notes, and telephone records, you could find not only tremendous success in the financial world but the glue that will hold the two of you together for life. And if, in addition, you can teach Virgo the art of spontaneity, you may be able to light a rare spark. The sensual but diffident Virgin may then relax your tension-ridden shoulders and give you the back rub of a lifetime. And not even you, with all your flightiness and head-in-the-clouds complacency, could refuse an offer like that.

Gemini with Libra

SEPTEMBER 24–OCTOBER 23

*L*ibra, ever seeking har-
mony, and represented by the balancing
scales of justice, is the most diplomatic,
soft-spoken, and fair-minded member of

the zodiac. This cardinal air sign, always a willing listener, will gently nudge you when you start to get lost in the labyrinthian corridors of your eloquence, and you should stop rambling long enough to pay close attention. Romantic, accommodating, and always delicate, Libra generally knows what it is doing, and the Scales will also have some enticing nonverbal rewards to offer.

The Scales, like you, will frequently

be found in the clouds, but Libra's pace is much slower. An air of classicism hovers about this elegant sign, and the Scales may be hard-pressed to keep up with your frenetic pace; so if your flighty attention wavers, you may leave your Libra behind. That would be a pity because the two of you could form a heavenly twosome that defies the laws of gravity.

You are the most social signs of the

zodiac, but whereas your energy is sometimes scattershot and diffuse, Libra's is
organized and coherent. The Scales net-
work relentlessly, and Libra will not be
happy unless it can converse with a dozen
different people from a dozen different
walks of life at the drop of a pin—or a
speed dialer. That beguiling charm will
complement your endearing tactlessness,
and the Scales will bring all of their for-
midable powers to bear upon making you

206

a success. With Libra on your arm, you will be a hit at every function, dinner, or formal ball you are required to attend. And when the party's over, Libra's sensual soul will continue to spin out magic and do wonders for your overactive mind. You two have so much in common that nothing, surely, could go wrong.

So it would seem, but both of you will have to be willing to bend somewhat and learn to march to the other's speed, or all of this limitless potential will go up in smoke. Eloquent speeches mean far less to the Scales than eloquent actions and the many things you share, and the quaint touches that you take for granted, or even may scorn, could make all the difference to this sentimental sign. *You* may think that buying little gifts or leaving love notes is silly and pointless, but Libra does not. So think of it as a game, the kind you so love to play (which Libra, in turn, considers silly and pointless), and you will have the Scales eating out of your hand.

Libra, after all, is ruled by Venus, so you will have to pass the test. If you can do so (but beware, because the Scales will be casting a very cold eye on your terror of commitment), this affectionate sign will colonize your heart and keep you happily at home. You will have to keep up your end of the bargain and be an agreeable partner in return; but considering the benefits that will cascade around you, that shouldn't be too difficult a task—especially since you are the most adaptable sign in the zodiac.

Gemini with Scorpio

OCTOBER 24–NOVEMBER 22

S*corpio is symbolized by*
the desert arachnid whose legendary sting
can kill, but the roller coaster would be almost as appropriate an emblem. If excite-

ment is what you've been searching for, then look no further than these seductive and penetrating eyes: They will provide the thrill of a lifetime. But don't forget to buckle up and stay buckled, because Scorpio is in the driver's seat. Make no mistake about *that*.

This fixed water sign is one of the most passionate and tempestuous in the zodiac, capable of maniacal fury, maniacal affection, and everything in between—and sometimes all of them at once. You will have to do all you can to help the Scorpion negotiate these storms; you will even be called upon to expose your innermost feelings. This sign, when it isn't threatening to sting you, may love you to death . . . but that sort of thing is anathema to you. You are the essence of intellectual spirit; Scorpio is the consummate emotional time bomb. In the end, your ways of looking at the world may simply prove impossible to reconcile.

If each of you can do your best to provide what the other lacks, however, you may have a chance to succeed. You, for example, could supply some needed objectivity to the self-obsessed Scorpion, a way of looking at situations with clarity and a refreshing lack of emotional baggage. If Scorpio can only see the kind of damage it unwittingly inflicts on those it cherishes, it may be able to try to mend its ways. And if *you* can pay a little more attention to the genuine agonies of others, instead of flying off whenever reality threatens, you might begin a growing process of your own. You are always an eager student of new ideas, so maybe you should approach this relationship as if it were a lesson to be learned—or a puzzle to be solved.

Friends may be perplexed: How can someone as carefree as you be drawn to a brooder like Scorpio? They have never been caught in those pincers; they have never been alone in the dark with so powerful a sign. When the Scorpion finally unveils all of its depths to you (which it will only do after it has chosen to trust you completely, which is a rare and, for this sign, almost impossible thing), you will be mesmerized as you have never been before or will ever be again. But it will only do that in private.

And it will never stop. That wild, unknown attraction between you will be difficult to break once it is formed—so if you have any of your customary doubts or hesitations, you had better depart now before you become involved. Hell hath no fury like a Scorpio scorned, which you could learn to your peril. And yet, long after most other signs have given up on you, Scorpio will lie there, with its piercing eyes and silent stare, drawing you out . . . and drawing you in. You could have no more captive an audience than a Scorpion in love, and what more could you ask for?

Gemini with Sagittarius

NOVEMBER 23–DECEMBER 21

The Archer who shoots

its idealistic arrows into the sky is your

polar opposite, or other half—mutable

fire to your mutable air. In certain

respects, however, you fit hand in glove because you are the perpetual student of the zodiac, and Sagittarius is the enduring teacher. You crave constant changes of scenery, and Sagittarius adores seeking out uncharted terrain. The thirst you both share for exploring new ideas and venues can take you all over the world even if you remain in your armchairs. But trouble still lurks in paradise.

You, after all, are a very quick

learner and a sponge for knowledge. Sagittarius is an equally adept instructor, so eventually there will come a time when you have learned all you can, and the Archer will have to adjust to you as an equal and not merely as a master instructing his disciple. If you can convince the Archer that it may have something to learn from *you*, however, then you may save the day. Sagittarius can then pick your brain for all those facts and bits of trivia that you have gleaned along the way from magazines, newspapers, or TV shows; and you might learn how to relate these to a larger pattern and no longer bog down in a swamp of useless data. The two of you could make a truly great team.

But if you both look constantly away from your base and into the great beyond, who will keep the home fires burning? Your restlessness makes it difficult for you to sit in one place for very long, but whereas you are merely jumpy and home late every night, Sagittarius is out of town, on business or on pleasure. You like being in and out all day; the Archer likes being in another place altogether. This may prove to be the ultimate riddle . . . yet you love nothing more than trying to solve a puzzle.

If you can do so, then you will have it made, because with Sagittarius coveting its freedom and you craving variety, the two of you will never feel crowded. Part of life's mystery revolves around the excitement of trying new things rather than wallowing in security, and this pair will ceaselessly explore. Just remember to make appointments to meet now and then, because you will both have some exciting stories to tell but may rarely have anyone to tell them to. If you can stop jabbering in your chatty way, and the

Archer can stop pontificating, those tales can continue between the sheets. There is no more exciting, adventurous, or dynamic a duo in the zodiac than the two of you when you are at your best, and your inspiration will be legendary. . . .

That is, as long as the Archer thinks it is directing the show. That could be another problem because you demand your own creative freedom. You will have to negotiate these shoals as well, but if you and Sagittarius can somehow manage to share center stage, the applause will last long into the night, even after the last curtain call is over and the audience has gone home.

Gemini with Capricorn

DECEMBER 22–JANUARY 20

This is the most serious, structured, and pessimistic member of the zodiac. A cardinal earth sign symbolized by the mountain goat slowly but surely ascending the ladder of success, Capricorn is totally responsible, remarkably honest, and the best friend anyone could have. Even if you only exchange handshakes with the Goat and not kisses, you will have a true companion for the rest of your life. And if you *do* become romantically involved, the Goat will never leave your side.

The two of you are as different as night and day, and that may be the perfect tie that binds. Your bubbly and optimistic personality will keep Capricorn spellbound and interested; the Goat will keep you tethered solidly to Earth. Whereas your lively and upbeat humor can bring shafts of light into the dour Goat's dark world, Capricorn, in turn, can bring seriousness to yours. Whereas you can effortlessly pull this sign into a realm of people, hopes, and visionary dreams, Capricorn can just as effectively give you one of its uncompromising stares and bring your flighty little games to an end. And whereas you come up with wonderful ideas that pop out of your brain just as quickly as they pop in, Capricorn can come up with a plan of action and transform those inspirations into reality. Finally you have just what you've always needed: someone who can put its money where your mouth is.

On the subject of money, the two of

you will flourish in business. You may be able to sweet-talk your way into a lucrative career or successfully market your product, but planning is beyond you, and cash pours through your fingers like sand. Steady and stable Capricorn is your diametrical opposite; when it comes to minding the financial store, you couldn't ask for a better manager. The Goat will carefully study trends and opportunities and prudently decide where to invest your profits, and Capricorn actually thinks of the future; you can't even bear the idea of looking a week in advance. This could be a dream come true—especially when you see how those canny investments have grown ten years down the line.

Nevertheless, as profoundly as you can enhance and uplift each other, you can also drag each other down. Your charm and reputation as a brilliant conversationalist means that you will be in constant demand on the party circuit and social scene. Capricorn may grow bitterly jealous, and ugly fights could ensue. Easy success could also go to your (already conceited) head, and because the Goat has to work so hard for everything it achieves, further resentment could fester. Your shallowness could also be an irritant, and Capricorn's heaviness could grate on your nerves.

Yet no sign is more loyal or reliable,

and it won't take much to keep your Goat happy. A little affection and attention will go a long, long way; and if you remember, as you are flirting and smiling at parties, that Capricorn is patiently waiting in the wings and would like to go home early, the Goat will gladly support you through life.

Gemini with Aquarius

JANUARY 21–FEBRUARY 19

Aquarius, *symbolized* by an angel pouring healing waters over the Earth, is serious, dedicated, responsible, otherworldly. This fixed air sign shares your predilection for flitting from one "social" gathering to the next, but its sense of political commitment is legendary, and most of its friends are also devoted to changing the world. Even though you are two of the most people-oriented signs of the zodiac, your aims and methods are radically different, and your paths might never cross.

Your activities will take you to media events, poetry readings, basketball games, or dinners with friends; the Water Bearer's will end up in political rallies, support groups, and strategy sessions. You are trying to have fun, and the fewer commitments the better; Aquarius is trying to save the planet, and too much is never enough. Even if you had something to talk about, you wouldn't have time because Aquarius is constantly on the go to a dozen different meetings, and you are constantly on the go; but in fact you have little in common.

Aquarius believes almost priggishly in honesty and fair play; you have always used words and ideas as foils with which to prick, cut, stab, or even parry, but rarely as instruments for uncovering truth. Aquarius is serious, forthright, and without humor; your lightsome sophistication, which may have masked (or atoned for) numerous pranks and lies when you were a child, will get you nowhere now when you are caught with your hands in the cookie jar. Aquarius has no time for excuses or long, involved fables; your glibness and ability to skate over thin ice will only land you in the drink now. And an Aquarian drink can be frigid.

Despite all this, however, the two of you are, in certain ways, kindred spirits. Both of you are air signs; both are more comfortable in the mind than in the heart. Neither has time for emotional trivialities or sentimentality (which can also serve as a neat excuse for avoiding serious emotional issues); and both of you even tend to suspect that, if you have to sit down and discuss intimacy, then the relationship is simply not working. All of these links, nevertheless, only bind you in your lack of connection. Your most common complaint may well be that you can't remember the last time you had dinner together; the Water Bearer's most common answer will be "I've been busy." The fact that you will now be on the receiving end of that uncomfortable old bromide is not likely to lighten your mood.

On the other hand, you will never know such unabashed freedom with any other sign. Others may provide the balance you need by pulling in the reins when you stray too far, but Aquarius will be the last one to lay down laws or set limits. And since both of you *are* air signs and great talkers, you should be able to sit across a table and discuss what you need to do to make this relationship work—if you've a mind to—and if you are together long enough in the house.

Gemini with Pisces

FEBRUARY 20–MARCH 20

Pisces, a mutable water sign symbolized by two fish swimming in opposite directions, is famous for its wavering and lack of fortitude. The Fish is astonishingly sensitive, kindhearted, and compassionate, a loving and trusting soul who will forgive almost anything you do so long as it believes that your intentions are pure. The Fish is insecure and highly empathetic, and can sympathize with anyone's confusions, uncertainties, or even strident attempts to bulldoze to a conclusion. The Fish is respectful and adoring: When it is obvious that someone (like a long-winded

Gemini) needs to be heard, Pisces will listen until you lose your voice. And the Fish's only weapon is to break your heart.

Leo will roar; Scorpio will lash out its stinger, but Pisces, when threatened or upset, will only swim away—or break down in tears. And because this is by the far the most sensitive member of the zodiac, anyone can hurt its vulnerable feelings with a minimum of effort. *You,* for whom sarcasm is not only a weapon but a proudly brandished badge of superiority, will hurt the Fish all the time, even when you don't mean to. And sometimes you do. You will grow impatient with the Piscean genius for wavering and avoiding confrontation, and on those occasions you will prick deliberately for a reaction. It will come in a cascade of sobs, and then you will regret too late what you have done. Few things distress you as much as watching someone cry.

246

And no vision is more haunting than the hurtful stare of a wounded Fish.

The contrast is stark: You use your brain and Pisces, its heart; you love throwing the verbal darts that rip Pisces to pieces. The very severity of your differences may be your only hope—but the two of you will have to play an intricate game of give-and-take.

The Fish can ask you to help bring clarity to its turbulent world and to provide a pathway out of its hysteria, and you can ask Pisces to help draw out your deeper emotions and to open the door to your heart and soul. Few signs could reach you in that special way, so save your sharp tongue for the appropriate occasions. It is unnecessary, and indeed gratuitous, around Pisces—and when push comes to shove, wouldn't you infinitely rather be in that watery, loving embrace? Only a fool would say no.

The only danger is that the two of you might never grow up. Pisces is a poetic dreamer whose head is constantly in the waves, and you are closer to Peter Pan than to anyone else, so the two of you could move to never-never land without thinking twice—and without ever moving out. That penchant for fantasy and childish dislike of the real world, however, may be your strongest bond. If you can at least return to Earth long enough to pay the bills occasionally, or to clean up the house, you will already have gained something. And with the sweetest sign of the zodiac in your arms, you may well need nothing more.

You and the
the
Moon

*J*ust *as the Moon takes a* month to orbit the Earth, so it requires approximately thirty days to pass through, or transit, the various signs of the zodiac—beginning with Aries, ending with Pisces, and spending about two and a half days in each. As it does so, it exerts an extraordinary influence on our moods, much as it expends a mysterious,

254

physical pull on the ocean's tides.

The Sun may guide our more conscious and overt qualities, but the Moon
rules over our instinctive, intuitive life;
when we examine our daily moon signs,
we become aware of the myriad and mys-
tical ways in which that lunar body
affects our emotional weather. When it
transits a fire sign, for example, we are
often dominated by fiery emotions, such
as anger and passion. As it moves to an

earth sign, we will feel a more rooted need for stability and comfort. The Moon in a water sign will generally bring watery emotions, like sadness and confusion; and an air-sign passage will lead to a sharpening of our thirst for knowledge.

Obviously, emotional weather isn't identical for everyone; the relationship between the position of the Moon and your particular sun sign will influence what the precise mood of the moment will be for you, and a constant subtle interplay occurs. If we pay close attention to the passages of the Moon, however, we can become far more adept at negotiating wisely and well the many challenges and changes of our daily life.

(Consult the moon charts beginning on page 332 for the time and date that the Moon enters each of the twelve signs of the zodiac throughout every month of the year from 1997 to 2005.)

The Moon in Aries

The god of war rules Aries, so when the Moon slips into these uncharted waters, you may think you've been transported to the heart of darkness. Danger and excitement will lurk around every corner; electricity and independence will rule the air. Lightning bolts will burst through you, and this challenging, temperamental Moon will only heighten your restless need to *constantly* try something new. In a change from your usual pattern, however, this particular influence may actually lend you some focus to complement your speed. Normally you vacillate and intellectualize before marching on, but the hyperkinetic Aries Moon will change all that for the better.

If you are single, love may crack you across the face during this transit, even though you usually remain aloof until boxed into a corner and forced to make up your mind. The Aries Moon will be a breath of fresh air in this regard, and for the next few days you will no longer be in sole control of your life. Don't worry about it; accept any and every social invitation because the man or woman of your dreams may join you at the piano or be sitting at the bar. Try the canapés, dip into the punch bowl, plunge into the swimming pool. Romance could find you anywhere.

If you are already attached, arrange a special night out on the town with those you love, because you do not want to be trapped at home during this active and outgoing transit . . . and the evening doesn't have to end when everyone else says good night. The Aries Moon is a highly libidinous one, so these two and a half days should be very sweet indeed. Try new variations; return to old approaches with a piquant spin, and tell your partner to expect a series of treats.

But also be sure to warn those closest to you not to pick a fight during this highly aggressive passage, because your always-sharp tongue will be razorlike now if anyone should disagree with you even slightly. Let an actual argument ensue, and your poisonous verbal arrows might become radioactive. Fortunately, your glib tongue *could* allow you to talk yourself out of a potential blowup—but with the Moon in Aries to accentuate your own flightiness, there are absolutely no guarantees.

The Moon in Taurus

The Moon *is exalted,* or most comfortable, in Taurus, so during this transit your emotions will stabilize and your mind should be at peace. Now you can take a break from the exhilarating frenzy that gripped you under Aries—but although many people would find this quiet passage a relief, you may well consider it boring and confining. You will have to get used to it nevertheless, for no matter where you turn, you will feel that your energy has been depleted—and anyone who so thrives on excitement and continual movement will have difficulty adjusting. Why not go to the video store and relax with a musical or comedy? At least you'll feel upbeat, if temporarily uprooted. You may even impress that special someone with your wonderful impersonations or sing-along skills.

No matter how laid-back you may feel, you will never be too tired for flirtations and the excitement of a new romance; and as your talkative and clever qualities align with sensual and gentle Taurus, you should easily be able to keep that new attraction entertained by day ... and comforted by night. You may even form a relationship with someone at work or with whom you could begin a lucrative business partnership. Patience and understanding will be abundant under the Taurus Moon, and they will also help endear you to others.

If you are already attached, your newly discovered sensitivity will surprise—and please—whoever shares your most intimate moments. This Moon will also improve your attention span, at least for a few days, so you may actually even listen to what your mate has to say. What a novel idea! How impressive and flattering! But you should alert your partner to seize as much of the day as possible now because the Moon will enter your own sign next, and once that happens you will never stop, listen, or shut up.

And you yourself should take full

advantage of your financial opportunities because the Taurus Moon is exceedingly savvy in this regard, and now would be an excellent time to earn money on a prior investment, buy a lottery ticket, or even ask for a well-deserved promotion. But don't put all your eggs in one basket because the upcoming Gemini Moon may snatch them away just as easily as Taurus provides them.

The Moon in Gemini

What would it be like to start the day with ten cups of coffee? Once the Moon passes into Gemini, you won't have to ask. You are already restless, nervous, and high-strung, but so much energy will shoot through you now that you may have to take a hot bath or warm glass of milk in order to wind down enough to *try* to get some rest at night (don't bank on much; you may not sleep again until the Moon transits Cancer). And if you have even the vaguest notion of what "relaxation" means, you should try to cultivate it. If not, you'd better learn.

Love will be tough because, although

you may hum with energy, you will find it impossible to stay in one place for very long. Your voluble powers of conversation could spin out of control, and your attention span (your what?) will take a trip to Mars. Rather than try to impress a new date with dinner, therefore, you might consider a night of dancing to help you work off that excess energy. You'll be so hyperactive during this transit that you won't be able to sit through a meal, and would only drive your new love interest mad.

If you are already committed, you'd better warn your partner that you will be moody and on edge for the next few days, and that the best thing would be to leave you alone. Though this may prove difficult, the alternative would be even worse because *no one* should be around you when the sparks start to fly. Even you may have trouble.

Save your brilliant ideas for work,

play, anywhere but home: Your colleagues
and friends will be dutifully impressed by
the flares that constantly shoot from you
over the next two or three days. At the
same time, you should try to be as thor-
ough and organized as you can (transla-
tion: buy a notebook and write it all
down), because you are not good at
follow-through in the best of times, and
now you will be a disaster. You might not
even *remember* those shards of scintilla-

tion, let alone act on them; so don't hesitate to ask your support system for assistance. Otherwise you may be making excuses for your sloppiness rather than receiving praise for your innovation.

The Moon in Cancer

T he Moon rules Cancer, so when it traverses this secretive and maternal sign, you will become more sensitive to the world around you, and so will everyone else. The influence of the retiring Crab will make you moody, un-predictable, and unable to make up your mind; and since you tend to vacillate in any case, this would not be the best time for you to make appointments or set up dates: You would only have to cancel them at the last moment. On the other hand, Cancer's artistic influence could give a boost to your already unique and innovative mind. Imagination will be ex-alted, so get to work on completing any creative endeavors you may have begun when the Moon was in Gemini. Now you will be in top form.

You will be equally sublime on the amorous front, so take advantage of this wonderfully dreamy transit by professing your love to someone who might not even catch your eye under a less romantic Moon. Normally you're a wizard at conversational chitchat and hopeless when it comes to the real thing, but not now. To your own amazement, you may find your-self uttering words like "marriage," "commitment," "home," and "family"; so if you've been attempting to broach such subjects with that special someone, but haven't found the appropriate time or phrases, this could be your moment. And if you begin now, the subsequent Leo Moon, which will burst with trumpet blares of romantic ardor, will only help you solidify and further your cause.

The Cancer Moon, like the Crab itself, constantly rides both the tip of the waves and the troughs, so if you are already committed, warn your mate that you may be more temperamental than usual. He or she will be used to your normal fluctuations by now, so these new ones might not even register. But they might also be overwhelming, so it is only fair to alert the public; and since Cancer is the sign of gourmet food and restaurants, you might suggest going out to an exotic dinner to fulfill the restless, romantic, and culinary urges that will assail you over the next few days. If solidifying your relationship is what you had in mind, these easy steps under this powerful and wavering Moon should certainly do the trick.

The Moon in Leo

Magnanimous *Leo is* ruled by the radiant Sun, and during this magnetic transit you will once again feel the heat of the spotlights and know that you are on center stage. Leo is the zodiac's greatest star, so this passage will call upon all of your deepest extroversion and desire to perform. If you have ever wanted to come out of the theatrical closet and reveal this side of yourself to others, this is the ideal time. Never will you feel more confident or bursting with creativity, and never will you find greater success. The world is your oyster, and you can do anything you want.

Professionally as well, this marvelously self-centered but generous passage can spur you to greater audacity and achievement, but it will exact a price. The Leo Moon will supply you with executive and organizational abilities to go along with your more vivid imagination, but it will also urge you to greater dominance and control. This will not exactly soften your already abrasive manner. On the other hand, the self-assurance you will gain from this transit could make you so appealing that prospective employers will fall over themselves to offer you jobs even if they have reservations about your ego. The same will be true in love.

The tremendously romantic Leo Moon will make you wildly attractive; and given the added dramatic qualities that you will also command, you will now possess the uncanny ability to convince a potential new partner that you are, indeed, such stuff as dreams are made of.

Your only real challenge will be to make the transition from flirtatious first date to lasting relationship; and because this is an issue with which you are constantly wrestling in any case, and because this intoxicating Moon is ill-suited to making such important long-term decisions, you should wait until the transit into Virgo before going any further. That prudent and sensible Moon can tell you whether or not this romance will be the real thing.

If you are already attached, this is the time for a weekend getaway to rediscover why you originally fell in love. The more spectacular and romantic the surroundings, the more loving and passionate the two of you will be. You will never find a better Moon to make all of your wishes come true.

The Moon in Virgo

Verbose and high-strung Mercury rules both Virgo and you, so during the next few days you may run around like a chicken with its head cut off. You will also be touchy and nervous,

so be sure to warn your friends that you
are operating on a very short fuse.
Indeed, you might even want to shelve
certain matters, no matter how pressing
or important, until the Moon exits this
edgy sign; for although the Virgin influence will lead to greater pragmatism than
the bombastic Leo Moon, it is also more
temperamental, and your judgment may
fluctuate. If you do happen to chew
somebody's ear off because you cannot

hold your temper, call upon Virgo's humility soon after to apologize.

Mercury was an asexual deity, so if you are single, a double dose of this Virginal influence is not likely to boost your chances of meeting the love of your life. It will, however, open up the door to hour upon hour of titillating conversation with family and friends; and because witty repartee is crucial to you, especially if you are seeking a permanent union, this Moon might induce you to fall in love with someone because of his or her mind—which would be a refreshing change. In that case, this pairing will not remain platonic for very long; and once the Moon transits romantic Libra, friendship could quickly turn to love.

If you are already committed, now is the hour to thrash out those issues that have been percolating for weeks, or even months, but which you have been unable to discuss because you never seem to have the time. Take advantage of the zodiac's most talkative Moon to *make* the time, because a better opportunity will never roll around.

Mercury also rules commerce, which means that buying and selling could be the order of the day. If you are thinking about investing in stocks and bonds, casting around for a new job, or even starting your own business, this would be the ideal moment to set the wheels in motion. The first step will be to find a nexus of talented people whose interests are in line with your own, and then man the phones. Networking will be at a premium during this transit, so lay as broad a foundation as you can.

The Moon in Libra

*L*ibra is an air sign like you, ruled by Venus, the goddess of love. During this ethereal transit, therefore, your desire to talk to anyone and everyone will be redoubled, but you will also be assailed by the need for romance, affection, and, last but not least, love. The Libra Moon will bring elegance and high spirit but little in the way of pragmatism, so your good sense (which was questionable to begin with) will go straight out the window, as will your impeccable timing. You may bog down in long-winded conversations in which you simply drone on, entranced by the sound of your own voice. On the other hand, you may also become enamored of someone else's.

This is perhaps the most loving, amorous, and sensual sign of the zodiac, so if you are unattached but are on the lookout, now is the perfect time to begin. Follow-through, however, which has always plagued you in any case, may be difficult because this is also the laziest constellation in the heavens. You may not do much; and your prey, who is also under the Libra Moon, may not respond

greatly even if you do. Tremendous per-
sistence will come with the Scorpio
Moon that follows, so if you can hold on
for the next few days, you can look for-
ward to a flying finish.

If you are already committed, be
sure to utilize the next few days to talk
over future plans—and, perhaps, diversions. Under the Libra Moon, you may
try to excise the tedious chores of your
everyday life and be transported to a

world of hopes, dreams, and ideas, which you may or may not ever put to practical use. Take this opportunity to map out a vacation in which you and your mate can have fun, relax, and, most of all, get back to the basics: Why were you attracted to each other in the first place? This is also the Moon of ultimate diplomacy, and no better moment will arrive to iron out any kinks that may have grown in your relationship . . . or to surprise your mate with an unexpected gift. It will not go unappreciated. "Sentimental" is the word of the moment, and anything that tugs at the heartstrings will be just what the doctor ordered.

The Moon in Scorpio

T*he Moon is fallen, or* weakened, in Scorpio—a brooding, wavering, and tempestuous sign—so that luminary's usual penchant for tenderness and sensitivity could suddenly turn to jealousy, anger, or perhaps, in extreme form, revenge; and even you, in all your detachment and smugness, will be forced to deal with your repressed but heartfelt emotions. There is no escaping the demands of this demanding Moon, so you might as well make the best of it.

If you are unattached and want to find a lasting partnership, you should try to maintain the sparkle that usually defines your personality despite the prickly seriousness of the Scorpio transit—although the combination of that new-found sobriety with your usual humor could prove more attractive than you might think. But try not to bombard your prospective love interest with the philosophical ruminations that will inevitably trail in the wake of the Scorpion's dominance: You are better off with cleverness and wit. A Gemini in top form is unlikely to be turned down.

If you are already involved, your partner will want to sit down and have a series of heart-to-heart talks in which you can finally straighten out all the many disagreements that have lingered in recent weeks. You, of course, would prefer to go to a movie and discuss it later, but that would only delay the inevitable: The Scorpio Moon requires the difficult and unpleasant ... which can also lead to useful reform. And you will have to accede because the intermingling of intense Scorpio and chatty Gemini will lead naturally to an emotional spring cleaning no matter what you do. Scorpio will also lend a monetary focus to the next several days, so be sure to take the time to review your finances and see how you can improve them.

The best thing this rigorous transit has to offer to someone like you is the incentive to start eating better and getting back into shape. Though you may well be one of those Twins who burn calories without even trying, you rarely give any real thought to your diet. Caffeine, nicotine, and fast-food restaurants are high on your "fun" list, so maybe you should take yourself to the local gym. This would also help prepare you for the energetic Sagittarius Moon, which lies directly ahead.

The Moon in Sagittarius

If *you really did begin* an exercise regime during the Scorpio transit, you will be in much better shape to withstand the highly athletic Sagittarius Moon. Socializing, networking, and party-going will be at an all-time high, so you will need exceptional energy to attend all the events to which you have been invited. And because important personal and professional contacts could be waiting in the wings, you should try to make every one of them.

If starting a new romance is high on your agenda, you could scarcely do better than the Sagittarius Moon, which is always seeking new adventures. Your own great gift of gab and the Sagittarian ability to be comfortable in any social situation should make you a shoo-in. Just make sure that whoever you meet can keep up with the exuberant pace you'll be setting over the next few days—and don't forget to slow down long enough to see who's lurking in the background. You might even attend a dance, go running in the park, or join a club in which other singles who share your interests may congregate. You wouldn't want to miss out on the opportunity of a lifetime.

If you are already attached, this could be a fantastic time for you and your mate to do something wildly exciting. Of course you could try new restaurants, or take in the arts, but you might find it even more intriguing to explore completely unknown terrain: Thailand, Barbados, or some obscure South Sea paradise you've never even heard of, let alone traveled to. This would not only satisfy the pioneering aspect of this transit (Sagittarius is the zodiac's great traveler), but also give the two of you time to take an overdue trip to a grand romantic location—something that you, amid all your busy affairs, have probably missed out on lately.

Indeed, the key for you during the Sagittarian transit is to open yourself up to all those experiences you have been craving but for which you have not found the time. The Archer is your zodiacal opposite; because each of you provides what the other lacks, you may feel as if an entirely new side of your personality has just opened up. Take advantage now, because when the Moon enters stodgy Capricorn, tight schedules will once again rule.

The Moon in Capricorn

Because the Moon is detrimental, or most uncomfortable, in Capricorn, feelings will take a backseat to action during the next few days. They always do with you in any case, so this could be a welcome influence in your life. Now would be an excellent time to take charge of any personal crises that may arise.

But you will have to contend with the practical and sobering side of this transit. Capricorn is ruled by Saturn, the Roman god of time, so although you may detest the clock in principle, this passage will force you to buckle down and cut back on your numerous activities.

With Capricorn rising, you may even be able to finish one or more of the projects you left hanging the last time something sexier suddenly caught your eye; and if you can manage to find a way to embrace this new influence, at least for the next few days, you may actually feel relieved and ready to inherit the whirlwind under Aquarius. Yes, you may just have to spend a few days organizing your files and cleaning your closet, but at least you can chat on the phone while you do these mundane tasks.

This Moon could finally be the answer to your prayers and help make up your mind about which prospective love interest you are going to choose. You may well have two (or more) clamoring for you, each with its own drawbacks and charms, and if anything can nudge you gently along, it will be the structured and disciplined mood that always hovers about the Goat. If you haven't noticed anyone interesting at your workplace thus far, take a second look. Capricorn is one of the most industrious signs of the zodiac, and this transit should make it easy for you to fall in love with someone who shares your professional outlook. Of course, you may be too busy catching up on projects at the office to even notice that special someone.

If you are already committed, this

could be the perfect time to solidify your relationship, either emotionally or legally. Stop dithering and be sure to compromise about whatever issues may have been bogging you down over the last few weeks. You may not enjoy sitting down to discuss monetary matters, but this would also be the ideal moment to pay your bills and plan your budget for the year ahead. The Moon moves into Aquarius and Pisces next, where reality will go straight out the window, so seize the day while it *means* something. This mood, too, will pass, and soon you'll begin your mad social whirl all over again.

The Moon in Aquarius

Aquarius, *however* utopian and eccentric, is also an air sign, so now you should be overjoyed to return to your own buoyant element, and you will want nothing more than to get out of the house and feel connected with the world once again. Dances, dinners, movies galore—and if you can't hop aboard the party circuit just yet, why not invite all your friends for a wild night at your place?

Veteran juggler though you be, even you may have trouble keeping up with all the appointments you have slated over the next few days. Professional obligations should be considerable, and you may also be bombarded by friends who crave a shoulder to cry on, or your wise and heartfelt advice; and because you are never one to turn down a pal in need, you may start tearing your hair out. Therefore, distasteful though the prospect may be, you might have to limit yourself to a handful of choice gatherings. After all, not even you can be in two places at once . . . though there is nothing in the world a Gemini would rather try.

This socially active and idealistic Moon should be very helpful to your love life, because if you meet someone at a favorite club or organizational event, you are already bound to have certain attitudes and interests in common. There is no better way to begin a relationship—though if the person you meet is as active and gadabout as you, you may have to communicate through answering machines for a while before you get a chance to connect. When you *do* make a date, you would be well-advised to wait until the Moon enters dreamy and romantic Pisces, when all systems will be go.

If you are already attached, you may wind up seeing your partner only briefly in the morning, or very late at night— and even the most practiced mate may boggle at the plethora of activities that plague you over the next few days. This is the group-activity Moon *par excellence*, which makes it all the more important that you whisk your partner away for at least a quick tête-à-tête, even if you have *no* time to spare. You do not want to forget who waits at home every night at the end of your busy days.

The Moon in Pisces

Pisces is the most imaginative, amorous, and unrealistic sign of the zodiac, so be prepared to throw reason and logic out the window during the next few days ... and to enjoy every minute. This is

not the time to contemplate important
moves or resolve long-standing problems
that require a methodical and carefully
crafted approach. (If anything, you will be
tempted to spend money foolishly, which
you will later regret.) Put decisions on the
back burner until a clearer-headed or more
action-oriented Moon comes along, which
it will do soon enough.

And you don't really enjoy the mundane practicalities of life in any case, so

glory in this delightful, if self-indulgent, Moon, whose flair for romance and even love at first sight are second to none— and may take over your life. The slightest touch could melt you; a silky voice can make you swoon, so surrender: It is the nature of the Fish. True, it is not your own: You are used to guarding, or even avoiding, your feelings, which you some- times suspect are beneath you. Now, however, you may be passing up the most golden opportunity of your life: candle-light dinners, midnight walks along the beach, oceans of sweet sentiment gently crashing against you. Ignore them now and you might regret it forever.

If you are already attached, you can now renew your mutual commitment with a dreamlike evening on the water, a spontaneous weekend in the country, a longer vacation atop an isolated mountain—anything that stirs the poetic soul.

Putting yourself second (always difficult for a Twin) and becoming completely attentive to your partner's every need will win you an unexpected, but delightful, favor in return. And you should try to keep this mood active even when the Moon enters Aries because you will once again be on the run, and you can build up a reservoir of goodwill now.

Professionally, you may be called upon to give even more than usual. This may also extend to volunteer activities and charitable organizations outside the home. If they are not already a part of your life, they may become so now. Pisces is the most generous and giving of signs, and the Pisces Moon could bring out reserves of altruism you never knew you possessed. And you will enjoy that too.

Moon Charts

1997–2005

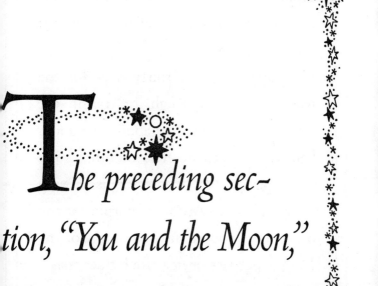

The preceding sec-
tion, "You and the Moon,"

explained in detail how the Moon affects your emotions and behavior as it moves through the twelve signs of the zodiac. It takes approximately thirty days for the Moon to pass through, or transit, the twelve signs—spending about two and a half days in each. So every month, for the short period that the Moon is moving through Leo, or Aries, or Scorpio (or any other sign), you can take advantage of the Moon's positive or negative influences.

The following charts show the date and time the Moon enters each sign of the zodiac. Just look up the current date (charts are provided for the years 1997 through 2005); the sign that precedes the date indicates the Moon's current transit. For instance, in the two following transits

Can Jan 10 19:43

Leo Jan 13 02:45

the Moon enters the sign of Cancer on

January 10 at 19:43 (7:43 P.M.) and stays in that sign until entering the sign of Leo on January 13 at 02:45 (2:45 A.M.). All times are eastern standard time in a twenty-four-hour clock format: 00:01–12:00 (noon) are the A.M. hours; 12:01–24:00 (midnight) are the P.M. hours (from 13:00 to 24:00, subtract 12 to translate into P.M.).

1997

	Sag Feb 01 23:49	Aqu Mar 05 14:53
Sco Jan 03 08:00	Cap Feb 04 03:43	Pis Mar 07 14:56
Sag Jan 05 14:26	Aqu Feb 06 04:20	Ari Mar 09 14:32
Cap Jan 07 16:54	Pis Feb 08 03:33	Tau Mar 11 15:38
Aqu Jan 09 16:59	Ari Feb 10 03:29	Gem Mar 13 19:49
Pis Jan 11 16:50	Tau Feb 12 05:56	Can Mar 16 03:51
Ari Jan 13 18:21	Gem Feb 14 11:54	Leo Mar 18 15:08
Tau Jan 15 22:40	Can Feb 16 21:12	Vir Mar 21 03:59
Gem Jan 18 05:53	Leo Feb 19 08:52	Lib Mar 23 16:34
Can Jan 20 15:28	Vir Feb 21 21:38	Sco Mar 26 03:41
Leo Jan 23 02:50	Lib Feb 24 10:22	Sag Mar 28 12:38
Vir Jan 25 15:26	Sco Feb 26 21:55	Cap Mar 30 19:06
Lib Jan 28 04:21	Sag Mar 01 07:00	Aqu Apr 01 22:57
Sco Jan 30 15:47	Cap Mar 03 12:37	Pis Apr 04 00:41

Ari Apr 06 01:19	Gem May 07 15:21	Leo Jun 08 14:58
Tau Apr 08 02:21	Can May 09 21:13	Vir Jun 11 02:43
Gem Apr 10 05:27	Leo May 12 06:32	Lib Jun 13 15:35
Can Apr 12 12:04	Vir May 14 18:43	Sco Jun 16 02:50
Leo Apr 14 22:22	Lib May 17 07:26	Sag Jun 18 10:37
Vir Apr 17 11:00	Sco May 19 18:11	Cap Jun 20 15:01
Lib Apr 19 23:35	Sag May 22 01:49	Aqu Jun 22 17:20
Sco Apr 22 10:17	Cap May 24 06:50	Pis Jun 24 19:08
Sag Apr 24 18:31	Aqu May 26 10:19	Ari Jun 26 21:38
Cap Apr 27 00:31	Pis May 28 13:17	Tau Jun 29 01:23
Aqu Apr 29 04:49	Ari May 30 16:17	Gem Jul 01 06:35
Pis May 01 07:49	Tau Jun 01 19:39	Can Jul 03 13:33
Ari May 03 09:59	Gem Jun 03 23:55	Leo Jul 05 22:45
Tau May 05 12:04	Can Jun 06 06:01	Vir Jul 08 10:22

Lib Jul 10 23:20	Sag Aug 12 04:44	Aqu Sep 12 23:08
Sco Jul 13 11:19	Cap Aug 14 10:40	Pis Sep 14 23:58
Sag Jul 15 20:01	Aqu Aug 16 12:57	Ari Sep 16 23:25
Cap Jul 18 00:44	Pis Aug 18 13:00	Tau Sep 18 23:22
Aqu Jul 20 02:28	Ari Aug 20 12:45	Gem Sep 21 01:39
Pis Jul 22 02:59	Tau Aug 22 13:58	Can Sep 23 07:33
Ari Jul 24 04:03	Gem Aug 24 17:56	Leo Sep 25 17:12
Tau Jul 26 06:53	Can Aug 27 01:11	Vir Sep 28 05:27
Gem Jul 28 12:04	Leo Aug 29 11:19	Lib Sep 30 18:32
Can Jul 30 19:38	Vir Aug 31 23:27	Sco Oct 03 06:57
Leo Aug 02 05:26	Lib Sep 03 12:29	Sag Oct 05 17:42
Vir Aug 04 17:15	Sco Sep 06 01:08	Cap Oct 08 02:02
Lib Aug 07 06:16	Sag Sep 08 11:53	Aqu Oct 10 07:28
Sco Aug 09 18:49	Cap Sep 10 19:22	Pis Oct 12 09:58

Ari Oct 14 10:24	Gem Nov 14 22:05	Leo Dec 16 17:57
Tau Oct 16 10:16	Can Nov 17 01:33	Vir Dec 19 03:59
Gem Oct 18 11:27	Leo Nov 19 08:38	Lib Dec 21 16:34
Can Oct 20 15:45	Vir Nov 21 19:32	Sco Dec 24 05:06
Leo Oct 23 00:10	Lib Nov 24 08:29	Sag Dec 26 15:06
Vir Oct 25 11:59	Sco Nov 26 20:42	Cap Dec 28 21:47
Lib Oct 28 01:04	Sag Nov 29 06:28	Aqu Dec 31 01:57
Sco Oct 30 13:14	Cap Dec 01 13:37	
Sag Nov 01 23:25	Aqu Dec 03 18:57	**1998**
Cap Nov 04 07:30	Pis Dec 05 23:06	Pis Jan 02 04:55
Aqu Nov 06 13:32	Ari Dec 08 02:23	Ari Jan 04 07:43
Pis Nov 08 17:34	Tau Dec 10 04:59	Tau Jan 06 10:52
Ari Nov 10 19:43	Gem Dec 12 07:35	Gem Jan 08 14:42
Tau Nov 12 20:45	Can Dec 14 11:25	Can Jan 10 19:43

Leo Jan 13 02:45	Lib Feb 14 08:17	Sag Mar 18 15:55
Vir Jan 15 12:31	Sco Feb 16 21:12	Cap Mar 21 01:41
Lib Jan 18 00:44	Sag Feb 19 08:55	Aqu Mar 23 08:00
Sco Jan 20 13:33	Cap Feb 21 17:29	Pis Mar 25 10:41
Sag Jan 23 00:23	Aqu Feb 23 22:08	Ari Mar 27 10:48
Cap Jan 25 07:38	Pis Feb 25 23:41	Tau Mar 29 10:06
Aqu Jan 27 11:25	Ari Feb 27 23:42	Gem Mar 31 10:38
Pis Jan 29 13:07	Tau Mar 02 00:01	Can Apr 02 14:10
Ari Jan 31 14:21	Gem Mar 04 02:15	Leo Apr 04 21:36
Tau Feb 02 16:24	Can Mar 06 07:26	Vir Apr 07 08:25
Gem Feb 04 20:09	Leo Mar 08 15:45	Lib Apr 09 21:04
Can Feb 07 01:57	Vir Mar 11 02:35	Sco Apr 12 09:55
Leo Feb 09 09:57	Lib Mar 13 14:57	Sag Apr 14 21:51
Vir Feb 11 20:09	Sco Mar 16 03:50	Cap Apr 17 08:04

Aqu Apr 19 15:40	Ari May 21 06:05	Gem Jun 21 16:26
Pis Apr 21 20:04	Tau May 23 07:05	Can Jun 23 18:38
Ari Apr 23 21:29	Gem May 25 07:25	Leo Jun 25 23:04
Tau Apr 25 21:08	Can May 27 08:59	Vir Jun 28 06:54
Gem Apr 27 20:55	Leo May 29 13:39	Lib Jun 30 18:04
Can Apr 29 22:58	Vir May 31 22:21	Sco Jul 03 06:45
Leo May 02 04:49	Lib Jun 03 10:16	Sag Jul 05 18:23
Vir May 04 14:47	Sco Jun 05 23:04	Cap Jul 08 03:26
Lib May 07 03:18	Sag Jun 08 10:33	Aqu Jul 10 09:51
Sco May 09 16:09	Cap Jun 10 19:49	Pis Jul 12 14:21
Sag May 12 03:47	Aqu Jun 13 03:02	Ari Jul 14 17:44
Cap May 14 13:37	Pis Jun 15 08:30	Tau Jul 16 20:33
Aqu May 16 21:29	Ari Jun 17 12:22	Gem Jul 18 23:18
Pis May 19 03:02	Tau Jun 19 14:47	Can Jul 21 02:43

Leo Jul 23 07:48	Lib Aug 24 10:02	Sag Sep 25 18:04
Vir Jul 25 15:34	Sco Aug 26 22:25	Cap Sep 28 05:29
Lib Jul 28 02:14	Sag Aug 29 10:54	Aqu Sep 30 13:51
Sco Jul 30 14:44	Cap Aug 31 21:21	Pis Oct 02 18:22
Sag Aug 02 02:47	Aqu Sep 03 04:19	Ari Oct 04 19:31
Cap Aug 04 12:16	Pis Sep 05 07:46	Tau Oct 06 18:57
Aqu Aug 06 18:30	Ari Sep 07 08:52	Gem Oct 08 18:43
Pis Aug 08 22:03	Tau Sep 09 09:16	Can Oct 10 20:49
Ari Aug 11 00:09	Gem Sep 11 10:40	Leo Oct 13 02:25
Tau Aug 13 02:04	Can Sep 13 14:20	Vir Oct 15 11:32
Gem Aug 15 04:45	Leo Sep 15 20:48	Lib Oct 17 23:02
Can Aug 17 08:55	Vir Sep 18 05:51	Sco Oct 20 11:36
Leo Aug 19 15:00	Lib Sep 20 16:57	Sag Oct 23 00:15
Vir Aug 21 23:21	Sco Sep 23 05:21	Cap Oct 25 12:03

Aqu Oct 27 21:42	Ari Nov 28 15:32	Gem Dec 30 02:21
Pis Oct 30 03:57	Tau Nov 30 16:51	
Ari Nov 01 06:26	Gem Dec 02 16:29	*1999*
Tau Nov 03 06:11	Can Dec 04 16:27	Can Jan 01 03:15
Gem Nov 05 05:10	Leo Dec 06 18:55	Leo Jan 03 05:30
Can Nov 07 05:39	Vir Dec 09 01:22	Vir Jan 05 10:50
Leo Nov 09 09:33	Lib Dec 11 11:43	Lib Jan 07 19:52
Vir Nov 11 17:36	Sco Dec 14 00:16	Sco Jan 10 07:48
Lib Nov 14 04:57	Sag Dec 16 12:46	Sag Jan 12 20:22
Sco Nov 16 17:40	Cap Dec 18 23:54	Cap Jan 15 07:27
Sag Nov 19 06:12	Aqu Dec 21 09:15	Aqu Jan 17 16:10
Cap Nov 21 17:44	Pis Dec 23 16:44	Pis Jan 19 22:39
Aqu Nov 24 03:42	Ari Dec 25 22:02	Ari Jan 22 03:24
Pis Nov 26 11:12	Tau Dec 28 01:03	Tau Jan 24 06:51

Gem Jan 26 09:28	Leo Feb 26 22:44	Lib Mar 30 20:49
Can Jan 28 11:56	Vir Mar 01 05:04	Sco Apr 02 07:48
Leo Jan 30 15:16	Lib Mar 03 13:34	Sag Apr 04 20:07
Vir Feb 01 20:37	Sco Mar 06 00:22	Cap Apr 07 08:38
Lib Feb 04 04:55	Sag Mar 08 12:45	Aqu Apr 09 19:23
Sco Feb 06 16:06	Cap Mar 11 00:52	Pis Apr 12 02:33
Sag Feb 09 04:37	Aqu Mar 13 10:30	Ari Apr 14 05:45
Cap Feb 11 16:09	Pis Mar 15 16:29	Tau Apr 16 06:06
Aqu Feb 14 00:55	Ari Mar 17 19:12	Gem Apr 18 05:38
Pis Feb 16 06:39	Tau Mar 19 20:08	Can Apr 20 06:27
Ari Feb 18 10:05	Gem Mar 21 21:05	Leo Apr 22 10:06
Tau Feb 20 12:28	Can Mar 23 23:34	Vir Apr 24 17:03
Gem Feb 22 14:53	Leo Mar 26 04:22	Lib Apr 27 02:46
Can Feb 24 18:08	Vir Mar 28 11:34	Sco Apr 29 14:12

Sag May 02 02:35	Aqu Jun 03 08:35	Tau Jul 07 10:20
Cap May 04 15:11	Ari Jun 08 00:06	Gem Jul 09 11:58
Aqu May 07 02:39	Tau Jun 10 02:42	Can Jul 11 12:27
Pis May 09 11:14	Gem Jun 12 02:47	Leo Jul 13 13:26
Ari May 11 15:51	Can Jun 14 02:14	Vir Jul 15 16:38
Tau May 13 16:55	Leo Jun 16 03:07	Lib Jul 17 23:20
Gem May 15 16:07	Vir Jun 18 07:12	Sco Jul 20 09:30
Can May 17 15:39	Lib Jun 20 15:10	Sag Jul 22 21:47
Leo May 19 17:36	Sco Jun 23 02:17	Cap Jul 25 10:07
Vir May 21 23:16	Sag Jun 25 14:50	Aqu Jul 27 20:53
Lib May 24 08:29	Cap Jun 28 03:10	Pis Jul 30 05:26
Sco May 26 20:04	Aqu Jun 30 14:18	Ari Aug 01 11:45
Sag May 29 08:36	Pis Jul 02 23:33	Tau Aug 05 18:56
Cap May 31 21:04	Ari Jul 05 06:20	Can Aug 07 20:52

Leo Aug 09 22:55	Lib Sep 10 17:15	Sag Oct 12 21:18
Vir Aug 12 02:21	Sco Sep 13 02:08	Cap Oct 15 10:02
Lib Aug 14 08:24	Sag Sep 15 13:34	Aqu Oct 17 22:15
Sco Aug 16 17:39	Cap Sep 18 02:12	Pis Oct 20 07:31
Sag Aug 19 05:31	Aqu Sep 20 13:36	Ari Oct 22 12:39
Cap Aug 21 17:59	Pis Sep 22 21:49	Tau Oct 24 14:24
Aqu Aug 24 04:48	Ari Sep 25 02:32	Gem Oct 26 14:33
Pis Aug 26 12:48	Tau Sep 27 04:49	Can Oct 28 15:09
Ari Aug 28 18:08	Gem Sep 29 06:20	Leo Oct 30 17:46
Tau Aug 30 21:39	Can Oct 01 08:31	Vir Nov 01 23:07
Gem Sep 02 00:24	Leo Oct 03 12:13	Lib Nov 04 06:56
Can Sep 04 03:09	Vir Oct 05 17:39	Sco Nov 06 16:45
Leo Sep 06 06:28	Lib Oct 08 00:51	Sag Nov 09 04:14
Vir Sep 08 10:56	Sco Oct 10 10:01	Cap Nov 11 16:59

Aqu Nov 14 05:44	Ari Dec 16 07:28	Ari Jan 12 13:46
Pis Nov 16 16:19	Tau Dec 18 11:43	Tau Jan 14 19:36
Ari Nov 18 22:55	Gem Dec 20 12:37	Gem Jan 16 22:23
Tau Nov 21 01:24	Can Dec 22 11:52	Can Jan 18 23:00
Gem Nov 23 01:13	Leo Dec 24 11:32	Leo Jan 20 22:58
Can Nov 25 00:29	Vir Dec 26 13:34	Vir Jan 23 00:07
Leo Nov 27 01:19	Lib Dec 28 19:14	Lib Jan 25 04:09
Vir Nov 29 05:10	Sco Dec 31 04:36	Sco Jan 27 12:01
Lib Dec 01 12:29		Sag Jan 29 23:17
Sco Dec 03 22:35	**2000**	Cap Feb 01 12:09
Sag Dec 06 10:27	Sag Jan 02 16:31	Aqu Feb 04 00:30
Cap Dec 08 23:12	Cap Jan 05 05:23	Pis Feb 06 11:00
Aqu Dec 11 11:57	Aqu Jan 07 17:52	Ari Feb 08 19:16
Pis Dec 13 23:15	Pis Jan 10 04:58	Tau Feb 11 01:19

Gem Feb 13 05:22	Leo Mar 15 16:42	Lib Apr 16 07:35
Can Feb 15 07:44	Vir Mar 17 19:48	Sco Apr 18 14:35
Leo Feb 17 09:11	Lib Mar 19 23:57	Sag Apr 20 23:57
Vir Feb 19 10:53	Sco Mar 22 06:17	Cap Apr 23 11:46
Lib Feb 21 14:21	Sag Mar 24 15:42	Aqu Apr 26 00:40
Sco Feb 23 20:58	Cap Mar 27 03:50	Pis Apr 28 12:04
Sag Feb 26 07:09	Aqu Mar 29 16:33	Ari Apr 30 19:53
Cap Feb 28 19:44	Pis Apr 01 03:10	Tau May 02 23:52
Aqu Mar 02 08:13	Ari Apr 03 10:20	Gem May 05 01:22
Pis Mar 04 18:29	Tau Apr 05 14:27	Can May 07 02:13
Ari Mar 07 01:52	Gem Apr 07 16:57	Leo May 09 04:01
Tau Mar 09 07:00	Can Apr 09 19:15	Vir May 11 07:40
Gem Mar 11 10:44	Leo Apr 11 22:15	Lib May 13 13:27
Can Mar 13 13:50	Vir Apr 14 02:18	Sco May 15 21:16

Sag May 18 07:09	Aqu Jun 19 14:25	Ari Jul 21 19:08
Cap May 20 19:00	Pis Jun 22 02:50	Tau Jul 24 02:42
Aqu May 23 07:59	Ari Jun 24 12:53	Gem Jul 26 07:00
Pis May 25 20:06	Tau Jun 26 19:17	Can Jul 28 08:28
Ari May 28 05:06	Gem Jun 28 21:57	Leo Jul 30 08:23
Tau May 30 10:00	Can Jun 30 22:08	Vir Aug 01 08:27
Gem Jun 01 11:33	Leo Jul 02 21:37	Lib Aug 03 10:32
Can Jun 03 11:29	Vir Jul 04 22:19	Sco Aug 05 16:04
Leo Jun 05 11:45	Lib Jul 07 01:47	Sag Aug 08 01:30
Vir Jun 07 13:57	Sco Jul 09 08:48	Cap Aug 10 13:43
Lib Jun 09 18:58	Sag Jul 11 19:05	Aqu Aug 13 02:42
Sco Jun 12 02:55	Cap Jul 14 07:27	Pis Aug 15 14:40
Sag Jun 14 13:18	Aqu Jul 16 20:25	Ari Aug 18 00:42
Cap Jun 17 01:26	Pis Jul 19 08:42	Tau Aug 20 08:29

Gem Aug 22 13:53	Leo Sep 23 01:59	Lib Oct 24 14:29
Can Aug 24 16:58	Vir Sep 25 04:01	Sco Oct 26 19:23
Leo Aug 26 18:16	Lib Sep 27 06:21	Sag Oct 29 02:40
Vir Aug 28 18:54	Sco Sep 29 10:30	Cap Oct 31 13:01
Lib Aug 30 20:33	Sag Oct 01 17:49	Aqu Nov 03 01:39
Sco Sep 02 00:56	Cap Oct 04 04:42	Pis Nov 05 14:11
Sag Sep 04 09:08	Aqu Oct 06 17:32	Ari Nov 08 00:00
Cap Sep 06 20:46	Pis Oct 09 05:35	Tau Nov 10 06:11
Aqu Sep 09 09:43	Ari Oct 11 14:49	Gem Nov 12 09:26
Pis Sep 11 21:32	Tau Oct 13 21:04	Can Nov 14 11:20
Ari Sep 14 06:59	Gem Oct 16 01:17	Leo Nov 16 13:18
Tau Sep 16 14:04	Can Oct 18 04:36	Vir Nov 18 16:15
Gem Sep 18 19:21	Leo Oct 20 07:41	Lib Nov 20 20:34
Can Sep 20 23:14	Vir Oct 22 10:52	Sco Nov 23 02:32

Sag Nov 25 10:32	Aqu Dec 27 16:24	Aqu Jan 23 22:42
Cap Nov 27 20:56	Pis Dec 30 05:26	Pis Jan 26 11:37
Aqu Nov 30 09:25		Ari Jan 28 23:33
Pis Dec 02 22:21	**2001**	Tau Jan 31 09:19
Ari Dec 05 09:15	Ari Jan 01 17:13	Gem Feb 02 15:54
Tau Dec 07 16:25	Tau Jan 04 01:54	Can Feb 04 18:59
Gem Dec 09 19:49	Gem Jan 06 06:43	Leo Feb 06 19:20
Can Dec 11 20:47	Can Jan 08 08:07	Vir Feb 08 18:34
Leo Dec 13 21:08	Leo Jan 10 07:43	Lib Feb 10 18:45
Vir Dec 15 22:30	Vir Jan 12 07:25	Sco Feb 12 21:52
Lib Dec 18 02:01	Lib Jan 14 09:05	Sag Feb 15 05:02
Sco Dec 20 08:11	Sco Jan 16 14:03	Cap Feb 17 15:58
Sag Dec 22 16:56	Sag Jan 18 22:36	Aqu Feb 20 04:53
Cap Dec 25 03:53	Cap Jan 21 09:56	Pis Feb 22 17:44

Ari Feb 25 05:19	Gem Mar 29 04:00	Leo Apr 29 18:24
Tau Feb 27 15:04	Can Mar 31 09:21	Vir May 01 21:15
Gem Mar 01 22:34	Leo Apr 02 12:52	Lib May 03 23:49
Can Mar 04 03:23	Vir Apr 04 14:45	Sco May 06 03:00
Leo Mar 06 05:29	Lib Apr 06 15:56	Sag May 08 08:05
Vir Mar 08 05:43	Sco Apr 08 18:00	Cap May 10 16:09
Lib Mar 10 05:46	Sag Apr 10 22:47	Aqu May 13 03:19
Sco Mar 12 07:42	Cap Apr 13 07:20	Pis May 15 16:00
Sag Mar 14 13:17	Aqu Apr 15 19:10	Ari May 18 03:39
Cap Mar 16 23:02	Pis Apr 18 07:59	Tau May 20 12:27
Aqu Mar 19 11:35	Ari Apr 20 19:16	Gem May 22 18:11
Pis Mar 22 00:27	Tau Apr 23 03:54	Can May 24 21:41
Ari Mar 24 11:42	Gem Apr 25 10:10	Leo May 27 00:11
Tau Mar 26 20:49	Can Apr 27 14:48	Vir May 29 02:37

Lib May 31 05:40	Sag Jul 01 22:13	Aqu Aug 03 00:52
Sco Jun 02 09:56	Cap Jul 04 07:21	Pis Aug 05 13:29
Sag Jun 04 15:57	Aqu Jul 06 18:32	Ari Aug 08 02:03
Cap Jun 07 00:23	Pis Jul 09 07:04	Tau Aug 10 13:21
Aqu Jun 09 11:19	Ari Jul 11 19:34	Gem Aug 12 21:56
Pis Jun 11 23:52	Tau Jul 14 06:12	Can Aug 15 02:53
Ari Jun 14 12:01	Gem Jul 16 13:23	Leo Aug 17 04:24
Tau Jun 16 21:37	Can Jul 18 16:55	Vir Aug 19 03:52
Gem Jun 19 03:40	Leo Jul 20 17:42	Lib Aug 21 03:18
Can Jun 21 06:40	Vir Jul 22 17:28	Sco Aug 23 04:49
Leo Jun 23 07:54	Lib Jul 24 18:07	Sag Aug 25 09:59
Vir Jun 25 08:57	Sco Jul 26 21:17	Cap Aug 27 19:01
Lib Jun 27 11:10	Sag Jul 29 03:44	Aqu Aug 30 06:46
Sco Jun 29 15:28	Cap Jul 31 13:16	Pis Sep 01 19:31

Ari Sep 04 07:57	Gem Oct 06 10:10	Leo Nov 07 03:32
Tau Sep 06 19:16	Can Oct 08 17:18	Vir Nov 09 06:48
Gem Sep 09 04:39	Leo Oct 10 21:52	Lib Nov 11 08:52
Can Sep 11 11:07	Vir Oct 12 23:56	Sco Nov 13 10:44
Leo Sep 13 14:14	Lib Oct 15 00:25	Sag Nov 15 13:51
Vir Sep 15 14:38	Sco Oct 17 01:02	Cap Nov 17 19:39
Lib Sep 17 13:59	Sag Oct 19 03:47	Aqu Nov 20 04:54
Sco Sep 19 14:27	Cap Oct 21 10:12	Pis Nov 22 16:51
Sag Sep 21 18:01	Aqu Oct 23 20:26	Ari Nov 25 05:20
Cap Sep 24 01:48	Pis Oct 26 08:54	Tau Nov 27 16:04
Aqu Sep 26 13:04	Ari Oct 28 21:13	Gem Nov 30 00:02
Pis Sep 29 01:49	Tau Oct 31 07:46	Can Dec 02 05:29
Ari Oct 01 14:06	Gem Nov 02 16:11	Leo Dec 04 09:14
Tau Oct 04 00:59	Can Nov 04 22:42	Vir Dec 06 12:10

Lib Dec 08 14:56	Lib Jan 04 20:23	Sag Feb 05 10:21
Sco Dec 10 18:08	Sco Jan 06 23:41	Cap Feb 07 18:07
Sag Dec 12 22:29	Sag Jan 09 04:57	Aqu Feb 10 04:14
Cap Dec 15 04:47	Cap Jan 11 12:18	Pis Feb 12 15:52
Aqu Dec 17 13:43	Aqu Jan 13 21:41	Ari Feb 15 04:24
Pis Dec 20 01:09	Pis Jan 16 08:59	Tau Feb 17 16:57
Ari Dec 22 13:44	Ari Jan 18 21:34	Gem Feb 20 03:48
Tau Dec 25 01:10	Tau Jan 21 09:45	Can Feb 22 11:13
Gem Dec 27 09:37	Gem Jan 23 19:26	Leo Feb 24 14:34
Can Dec 29 14:38	Can Jan 26 01:15	Vir Feb 26 14:45
Leo Dec 31 17:08	Leo Jan 28 03:29	Lib Feb 28 13:46
	Vir Jan 30 03:39	Sco Mar 02 13:52
2002	Lib Feb 01 03:44	Sag Mar 04 16:54
Vir Jan 02 18:33	Sco Feb 03 05:34	Cap Mar 06 23:48

356

Aqu Mar 09 09:56	Ari Apr 10 16:39	Gem May 12 22:03
Pis Mar 11 21:56	Tau Apr 13 04:54	Can May 15 06:32
Ari Mar 14 10:33	Gem Apr 15 15:55	Leo May 17 12:50
Tau Mar 16 22:59	Can Apr 18 00:59	Vir May 19 16:59
Gem Mar 19 10:18	Leo Apr 20 07:19	Lib May 21 19:17
Can Mar 21 19:05	Vir Apr 22 10:33	Sco May 23 20:37
Leo Mar 24 00:10	Lib Apr 24 11:20	Sag May 25 22:19
Vir Mar 26 01:42	Sco Apr 26 11:15	Cap May 28 01:54
Lib Mar 28 01:03	Sag Apr 28 12:13	Aqu May 30 08:34
Sco Mar 30 00:21	Cap Apr 30 16:02	Pis Jun 01 18:36
Sag Apr 01 01:49	Aqu May 02 23:44	Ari Jun 04 06:50
Cap Apr 03 06:58	Pis May 05 10:45	Tau Jun 06 19:05
Aqu Apr 05 16:06	Ari May 07 23:21	Gem Jun 09 05:28
Pis Apr 08 03:57	Tau May 10 11:30	Can Jun 11 13:13

Leo Jun 13 18:38	Lib Jul 15 06:38	Sag Aug 15 18:24
Vir Jun 15 22:22	Sco Jul 17 09:12	Cap Aug 18 00:15
Lib Jun 18 01:10	Sag Jul 19 13:02	Aqu Aug 20 08:16
Sco Jun 20 03:41	Cap Jul 21 18:25	Pis Aug 22 18:10
Sag Jun 22 06:41	Aqu Jul 24 01:39	Ari Aug 25 05:46
Cap Jun 24 11:01	Pis Jul 26 11:04	Tau Aug 27 18:30
Aqu Jun 26 17:35	Ari Jul 28 22:38	Gem Aug 30 06:44
Pis Jun 29 03:00	Tau Jul 31 11:15	Can Sep 01 16:12
Ari Jul 01 14:48	Gem Aug 02 22:44	Leo Sep 03 21:34
Tau Jul 04 03:15	Can Aug 05 07:00	Vir Sep 05 23:14
Gem Jul 06 13:58	Leo Aug 07 11:25	Lib Sep 07 22:56
Can Jul 08 21:34	Vir Aug 09 13:02	Sco Sep 09 22:48
Leo Jul 11 02:06	Lib Aug 11 13:37	Sag Sep 12 00:44
Vir Jul 13 04:39	Sco Aug 13 15:00	Cap Sep 14 05:47

Aqu Sep 16 13:54	Ari Oct 18 18:12	Gem Nov 20 01:23
Pis Sep 19 00:17	Tau Oct 21 06:55	Can Nov 22 11:46
Ari Sep 21 12:10	Gem Oct 23 19:16	Leo Nov 24 19:58
Tau Sep 24 00:53	Can Oct 26 06:09	Vir Nov 27 01:40
Gem Sep 26 13:25	Leo Oct 28 14:18	Lib Nov 29 04:53
Can Sep 28 23:59	Vir Oct 30 18:58	Sco Dec 01 06:14
Leo Oct 01 06:57	Lib Nov 01 20:27	Sag Dec 03 06:57
Vir Oct 03 09:50	Sco Nov 03 20:09	Cap Dec 05 08:38
Lib Oct 05 09:50	Sag Nov 05 20:01	Aqu Dec 07 12:54
Sco Oct 07 08:57	Cap Nov 07 21:59	Pis Dec 09 20:46
Sag Oct 09 09:21	Aqu Nov 10 03:27	Ari Dec 12 07:57
Cap Oct 11 12:45	Pis Nov 12 12:41	Tau Dec 14 20:42
Aqu Oct 13 19:51	Ari Nov 15 00:37	Gem Dec 17 08:41
Pis Oct 16 06:06	Tau Nov 17 13:22	Can Dec 19 18:29

Leo Dec 22 01:47	Leo Jan 18 09:27	Lib Feb 18 23:47
Vir Dec 24 07:04	Vir Jan 20 13:30	Sco Feb 21 01:09
Lib Dec 26 10:52	Lib Jan 22 16:22	Sag Feb 23 03:45
Sco Dec 28 13:40	Sco Jan 24 19:08	Cap Feb 25 08:10
Sag Dec 30 16:00	Sag Jan 26 22:25	Aqu Feb 27 14:24
	Cap Jan 29 02:29	Pis Mar 01 22:25
2003	Aqu Jan 31 07:44	Ari Mar 04 08:29
Cap Jan 01 18:42	Pis Feb 02 14:54	Tau Mar 06 20:35
Aqu Jan 03 22:57	Ari Feb 05 00:44	Gem Mar 09 09:36
Pis Jan 06 05:56	Tau Feb 07 12:58	Can Mar 11 21:10
Ari Jan 08 16:14	Gem Feb 10 01:44	Leo Mar 14 05:05
Tau Jan 11 04:47	Can Feb 12 12:17	Vir Mar 16 08:51
Gem Jan 13 17:06	Leo Feb 14 19:03	Lib Mar 18 09:42
Can Jan 16 02:54	Vir Feb 16 22:21	Sco Mar 20 09:37

Sag Mar 22 10:33	Aqu Apr 23 01:58	Ari May 25 02:58
Cap Mar 24 13:48	Pis Apr 25 10:02	Tau May 27 15:31
Aqu Mar 26 19:50	Ari Apr 27 20:54	Gem May 30 04:30
Pis Mar 29 04:25	Tau Apr 30 09:25	Can Jun 01 16:26
Ari Mar 31 15:04	Gem May 02 22:26	Leo Jun 04 02:23
Tau Apr 03 03:19	Can May 05 10:40	Vir Jun 06 09:49
Gem Apr 05 16:23	Leo May 07 20:44	Lib Jun 08 14:28
Can Apr 08 04:35	Vir May 10 03:29	Sco Jun 10 16:37
Leo Apr 10 13:51	Lib May 12 06:41	Sag Jun 12 17:11
Vir Apr 12 19:05	Sco May 14 07:12	Cap Jun 14 17:37
Lib Apr 14 20:40	Sag May 16 06:42	Aqu Jun 16 19:41
Sco Apr 16 20:15	Cap May 18 07:03	Pis Jun 19 00:57
Sag Apr 18 19:51	Aqu May 20 10:01	Ari Jun 21 10:05
Cap Apr 20 21:20	Pis May 22 16:40	Tau Jun 23 22:14

Gem Jun 26 11:11	Leo Jul 28 15:15	Lib Aug 29 08:40
Can Jun 28 22:50	Vir Jul 30 21:25	Sco Aug 31 10:59
Leo Jul 01 08:12	Lib Aug 02 01:46	Sag Sep 02 13:31
Vir Jul 03 15:14	Sco Aug 04 05:11	Cap Sep 04 16:50
Lib Jul 05 20:19	Sag Aug 06 08:10	Aqu Sep 06 21:14
Sco Jul 07 23:42	Cap Aug 08 11:02	Pis Sep 09 03:06
Sag Jul 10 01:47	Aqu Aug 10 14:23	Ari Sep 11 11:09
Cap Jul 12 03:20	Pis Aug 12 19:18	Tau Sep 13 21:49
Aqu Jul 14 05:37	Ari Aug 15 03:00	Gem Sep 16 10:31
Pis Jul 16 10:14	Tau Aug 17 13:52	Can Sep 18 23:06
Ari Jul 18 18:18	Gem Aug 20 02:40	Leo Sep 21 09:01
Tau Jul 21 05:47	Can Aug 22 14:43	Vir Sep 23 15:02
Gem Jul 23 18:41	Leo Aug 24 23:46	Lib Sep 25 17:48
Can Jul 26 06:22	Vir Aug 27 05:25	Sco Sep 27 18:51

Sag Sep 29 19:56	Aqu Oct 31 08:41	Ari Dec 02 05:55
Cap Oct 01 22:21	Pis Nov 02 14:52	Tau Dec 04 17:29
Aqu Oct 04 02:45	Ari Nov 05 00:02	Gem Dec 07 06:25
Pis Oct 06 09:20	Tau Nov 07 11:28	Can Dec 09 19:10
Ari Oct 08 18:07	Gem Nov 10 00:13	Leo Dec 12 06:39
Tau Oct 11 05:04	Can Nov 12 13:09	Vir Dec 14 16:05
Gem Oct 13 17:44	Leo Nov 15 00:46	Lib Dec 16 22:44
Can Oct 16 06:40	Vir Nov 17 09:34	Sco Dec 19 02:18
Leo Oct 18 17:40	Lib Nov 19 14:40	Sag Dec 21 03:14
Vir Oct 21 00:59	Sco Nov 21 16:22	Cap Dec 23 02:55
Lib Oct 23 04:25	Sag Nov 23 16:02	Aqu Dec 25 03:13
Sco Oct 25 05:07	Cap Nov 25 15:31	Pis Dec 27 06:09
Sag Oct 27 04:54	Aqu Nov 27 16:48	Ari Dec 29 13:09
Cap Oct 29 05:36	Pis Nov 29 21:26	

2004

Tau Jan 01 00:01	Gem Jan 30 20:17	Leo Mar 03 04:16
Gem Jan 03 12:57	Can Feb 02 09:02	Vir Mar 05 12:16
Can Jan 06 01:37	Leo Feb 04 19:49	Lib Mar 07 17:30
Leo Jan 08 12:37	Vir Feb 07 04:01	Sco Mar 09 21:02
Vir Jan 10 21:36	Lib Feb 09 10:11	Sag Mar 11 23:56
Lib Jan 13 04:37	Sco Feb 11 14:56	Cap Mar 14 02:51
Sco Jan 15 09:31	Sag Feb 13 18:34	Aqu Mar 16 06:09
Sag Jan 17 12:16	Cap Feb 15 21:13	Pis Mar 18 10:26
Cap Jan 19 13:23	Aqu Feb 17 23:27	Ari Mar 20 16:28
Aqu Jan 21 14:10	Pis Feb 20 02:27	Tau Mar 23 01:09
Pis Jan 23 16:28	Ari Feb 22 07:45	Gem Mar 25 12:34
Ari Jan 25 22:06	Tau Feb 24 16:30	Can Mar 28 01:22
Tau Jan 28 07:46	Gem Feb 27 04:22	Leo Mar 30 13:05
	Can Feb 29 17:11	Vir Apr 01 21:43

Lib Apr 04 02:50	Sag May 05 16:07	Aqu Jun 06 02:10
Sco Apr 06 05:23	Cap May 07 16:16	Pis Jun 08 04:38
Sag Apr 08 06:49	Aqu May 09 17:45	Ari Jun 10 10:50
Cap Apr 10 08:33	Pis May 11 21:52	Tau Jun 12 20:36
Aqu Apr 12 11:33	Ari May 14 05:02	Gem Jun 15 08:43
Pis Apr 14 16:23	Tau May 16 14:56	Can Jun 17 21:36
Ari Apr 16 23:24	Gem May 19 02:46	Leo Jun 20 10:03
Tau Apr 19 08:42	Can May 21 15:34	Vir Jun 22 21:08
Gem Apr 21 20:09	Leo May 24 04:06	Lib Jun 25 05:49
Can Apr 24 08:55	Vir May 26 14:50	Sco Jun 27 11:10
Leo Apr 26 21:13	Lib May 28 22:20	Sag Jun 29 13:14
Vir Apr 29 06:59	Sco May 31 02:06	Cap Jul 01 13:00
Lib May 01 13:00	Sag Jun 02 02:51	Aqu Jul 03 12:22
Sco May 03 15:37	Cap Jun 04 02:12	Pis Jul 05 13:27

Ari Jul 07 18:02	Gem Aug 08 21:32	Leo Sep 10 06:05
Tau Jul 10 02:50	Can Aug 11 10:19	Vir Sep 12 16:15
Gem Jul 12 14:44	Leo Aug 13 22:28	Lib Sep 14 23:52
Can Jul 15 03:40	Vir Aug 16 08:48	Sco Sep 17 05:24
Leo Jul 17 15:55	Lib Aug 18 17:08	Sag Sep 19 09:28
Vir Jul 20 02:43	Sco Aug 20 23:35	Cap Sep 21 12:34
Lib Jul 22 11:37	Sag Aug 23 04:07	Aqu Sep 23 15:09
Sco Jul 24 18:07	Cap Aug 25 06:46	Pis Sep 25 17:55
Sag Jul 26 21:46	Aqu Aug 27 08:07	Ari Sep 27 21:57
Cap Jul 28 22:56	Pis Aug 29 09:33	Tau Sep 30 04:23
Aqu Jul 30 22:54	Ari Aug 31 12:46	Gem Oct 02 13:55
Pis Aug 01 23:35	Tau Sep 02 19:15	Can Oct 05 01:53
Ari Aug 04 03:00	Gem Sep 05 05:24	Leo Oct 07 14:22
Tau Aug 06 10:26	Can Sep 07 17:49	Vir Oct 10 00:58

Lib Oct 12 08:30	Sag Nov 13 00:55	Aqu Dec 14 11:10
Sco Oct 14 13:09	Cap Nov 15 01:32	Pis Dec 16 12:24
Sag Oct 16 15:57	Aqu Nov 17 02:39	Ari Dec 18 16:52
Cap Oct 18 18:06	Pis Nov 19 05:37	Tau Dec 21 00:52
Aqu Oct 20 20:37	Ari Nov 21 11:11	Gem Dec 23 11:32
Pis Oct 23 00:13	Tau Nov 23 19:15	Can Dec 25 23:37
Ari Oct 25 05:24	Gem Nov 26 05:24	Leo Dec 28 12:13
Tau Oct 27 12:37	Can Nov 28 17:10	Vir Dec 31 00:32
Gem Oct 29 22:11	Leo Dec 01 05:49	
Can Nov 01 09:52	Vir Dec 03 17:59	**2005**
Leo Nov 03 22:31	Lib Dec 06 03:45	Lib Jan 02 11:18
Vir Nov 06 09:58	Sco Dec 08 09:41	Sco Jan 04 18:58
Lib Nov 08 18:22	Sag Dec 10 11:52	Sag Jan 06 22:42
Sco Nov 10 23:03	Cap Dec 12 11:41	Cap Jan 08 23:09

Aqu Jan 10 22:07	Ari Feb 11 10:22	Gem Mar 15 08:44
Pis Jan 12 21:51	Tau Feb 13 15:18	Can Mar 17 19:43
Ari Jan 15 00:27	Gem Feb 16 00:18	Leo Mar 20 08:16
Tau Jan 17 07:06	Can Feb 18 12:12	Vir Mar 22 20:09
Gem Jan 19 17:23	Leo Feb 21 00:53	Lib Mar 25 05:59
Can Jan 22 05:41	Vir Feb 23 12:43	Sco Mar 27 13:27
Leo Jan 24 18:20	Lib Feb 25 22:57	Sag Mar 29 18:55
Vir Jan 27 06:23	Sco Feb 28 07:19	Cap Mar 31 22:47
Lib Jan 29 17:12	Sag Mar 02 13:28	Aqu Apr 03 01:30
Sco Feb 01 01:49	Cap Mar 04 17:11	Pis Apr 05 03:45
Sag Feb 03 07:20	Aqu Mar 06 18:48	Ari Apr 07 06:27
Cap Feb 05 09:30	Pis Mar 08 19:32	Tau Apr 09 10:50
Aqu Feb 07 09:25	Ari Mar 10 21:03	Gem Apr 11 17:54
Pis Feb 09 08:59	Tau Mar 13 01:06	Can Apr 14 04:03

Leo Apr 16 16:16	Lib May 18 23:28	Sag Jun 19 20:43
Vir Apr 19 04:26	Sco May 21 06:47	Cap Jun 21 21:51
Lib Apr 21 14:25	Sag May 23 10:36	Aqu Jun 23 21:36
Sco Apr 23 21:24	Cap May 25 12:10	Pis Jun 25 22:03
Sag Apr 26 01:44	Aqu May 27 13:09	Ari Jun 28 00:52
Cap Apr 28 04:32	Pis May 29 15:09	Tau Jun 30 06:44
Aqu Apr 30 06:53	Ari May 31 19:07	Gem Jul 02 15:25
Pis May 02 09:42	Tau Jun 03 01:19	Can Jul 05 02:07
Ari May 04 13:36	Gem Jun 05 09:35	Leo Jul 07 14:10
Tau May 06 19:01	Can Jun 07 19:46	Vir Jul 10 02:56
Gem May 09 02:28	Leo Jun 10 07:39	Lib Jul 12 15:08
Can May 11 12:20	Vir Jun 12 20:21	Sco Jul 15 00:49
Leo May 14 00:16	Lib Jun 15 07:57	Sag Jul 17 06:34
Vir May 16 12:45	Sco Jun 17 16:22	Cap Jul 19 08:25

Aqu Jul 2I 07:54	Ari Aug 2I I8:00	Gem Sep 22 12:07
Pis Jul 23 07:II	Tau Aug 23 20:58	Can Sep 24 2I:I0
Ari Jul 25 08:23	Gem Aug 26 03:43	Leo Sep 27 09:02
Tau Jul 27 12:55	Can Aug 28 13:57	Vir Sep 29 2I:43
Gem Jul 29 2I:02	Leo Aug 3I 02:I4	Lib Oct 02 09:23
Can Aug 0I 07:52	Vir Sep 02 I4:55	Sco Oct 04 I9:02
Leo Aug 03 20:09	Lib Sep 05 02:5I	Sag Oct 07 02:27
Vir Aug 06 08:53	Sco Sep 07 I3:09	Cap Oct 09 07:42
Lib Aug 08 2I:07	Sag Sep 09 2I:0I	Aqu Oct II II:04
Sco Aug II 07:33	Cap Sep I2 0I:55	Pis Oct I3 I3:04
Sag Aug I3 I4:45	Aqu Sep I4 04:0I	Ari Oct I5 I4:39
Cap Aug I5 I8:I2	Pis Sep I6 04:24	Tau Oct I7 I7:04
Aqu Aug I7 I8:38	Ari Sep I8 04:42	Gem Oct I9 2I:44
Pis Aug I9 I7:52	Tau Sep 20 06:47	Can Oct 22 05:40

Leo Oct 24 16:48	Lib Nov 26 01:56	Sag Dec 28 03:42
Vir Oct 27 05:27	Sco Nov 28 11:31	Cap Dec 30 06:34
Lib Oct 29 17:14	Sag Nov 30 17:31	
Sco Nov 01 02:27	Cap Dec 02 20:41	
Sag Nov 03 08:54	Aqu Dec 04 22:36	
Cap Nov 05 13:16	Pis Dec 07 00:44	
Aqu Nov 07 16:30	Ari Dec 09 04:02	
Pis Nov 09 19:22	Tau Dec 11 08:46	
Ari Nov 11 22:22	Gem Dec 13 14:59	
Tau Nov 14 02:02	Can Dec 15 23:01	
Gem Nov 16 07:09	Leo Dec 18 09:18	
Can Nov 18 14:42	Vir Dec 20 21:38	
Leo Nov 21 01:10	Lib Dec 23 10:25	
Vir Nov 23 13:41	Sco Dec 25 21:02	

This book was

typeset in Centaur and KuenstlerScript
by Sabrina Bowers.

Book design by

Judith Stagnitto Abbate and Junie Lee

374